PAPER TREES

genealogical clip-art

PAPER TREES

*genealogical
clip-art*

Tony Matthews

Published by Genealogical Publishing Co., Inc.
1001 N. Calvert St., Baltimore, MD 21202
Second printing, 1999
Third printing, 2004
Library of Congress Catalogue Card Number 98-75467
International Standard Book Number 0-8063-1607-1
Made in the United States of America

INTRODUCTION

Paper Trees is a unique collection of hand-drawn family trees and charts which you can fill in and color by yourself. All of these beautiful designs are original, and they are available as clip-art for use as cards, announcements, book covers, section dividers, reunion T-shirts and mugs, newsletter designs, research aids, or for any of a thousand other things.

Filled in by hand, calligraphy, or type, and hand-colored in pen or paint, each of these family trees is guaranteed to be unique, and each illustration—whether elegant, whimsical, or just plain folksy—is a joyful celebration of your family. Uses for it are limited only by your imagination.

You can photo-reduce the family trees for use as note cards and stationery, or you can enlarge them to show family detail at its optimum. Remember that each of these family trees is an *ancestral tree*. The tree starts with *you,* and each generation back doubles in size, showing two parents, four grandparents, eight great-grandparents, etc.

You'll have a great time with these illustrations, and you can pass them on finished or unfinished, to be treasured as keepsakes or to be embellished and completed by others.

Rules of Thumb

These family trees are all ancestral trees. Each generation back in time doubles in size—one of you, two parents, four grandparents, eight great-grandparents, etc.

The father always goes to the left.

Key

1. You
2. Your father
3. Your mother
4. Father of #2
5. Mother of #2
6. Father of #3
7. Mother of #3
8. Father of #4
9. Mother of #4
10. Father of #5
11. Mother of #5
12. Father of #6
13. Mother of #6
14. Father of #7
15. Mother of #7
16. Father of #8
17. Mother of #8
18. Father of #9
19. Mother of #9
20. Father of #10
21. Mother of #10
22. Father of #11
23. Mother of #11
24. Father of #12
25. Mother of #12
26. Father of #13
27. Mother of #13
28. Father of #14
29. Mother of #14
30. Father of #15
31. Mother of #15

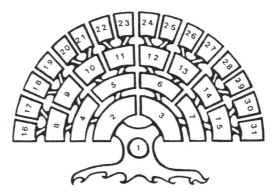

Variations

Instead of YOU, put:

- the family surname
- the wedding date of the father and mother
- the names of all the children

PAPER TREES

genealogical clip-art

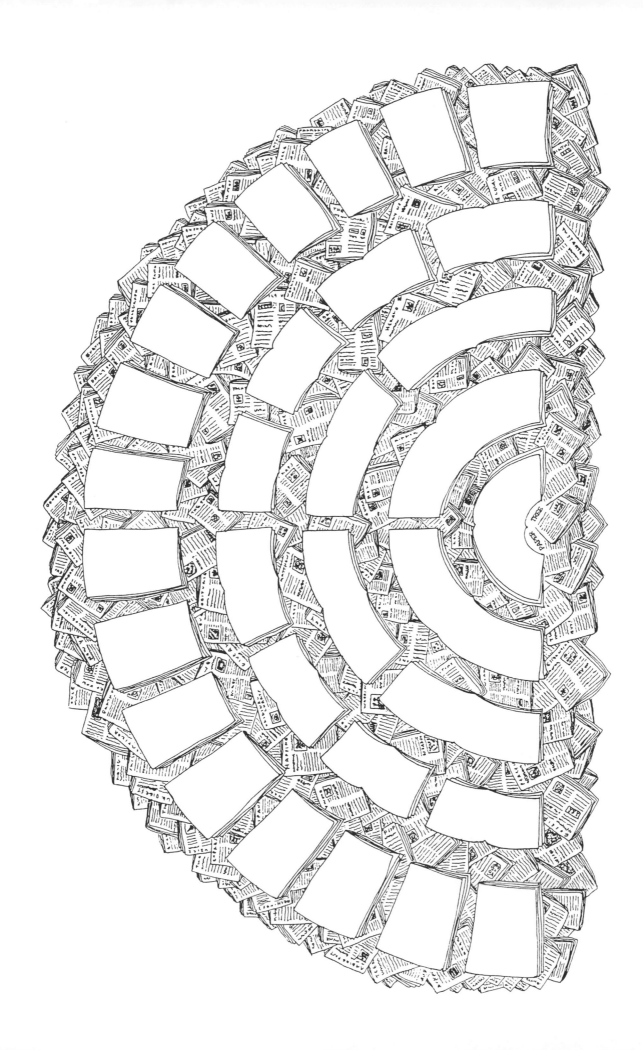

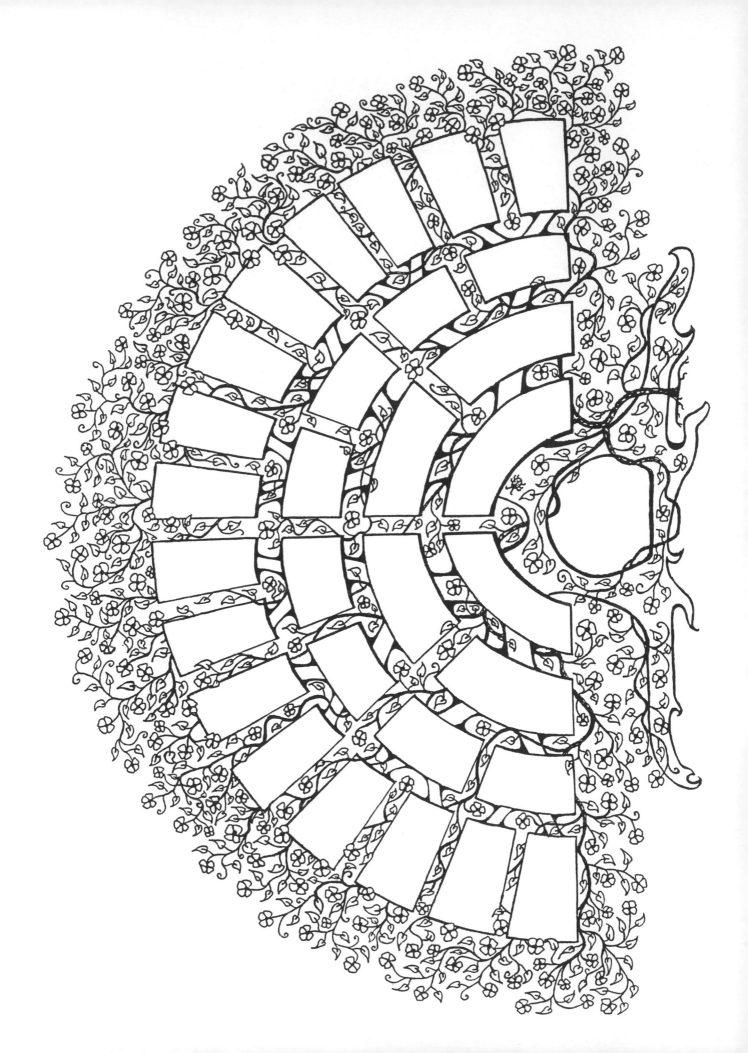

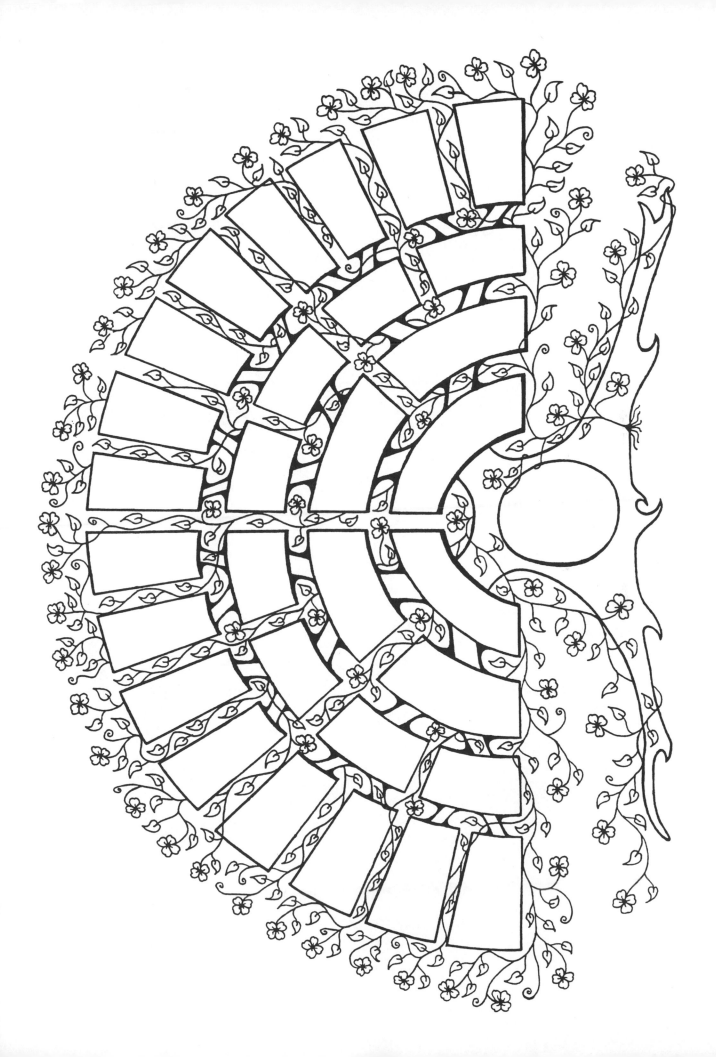

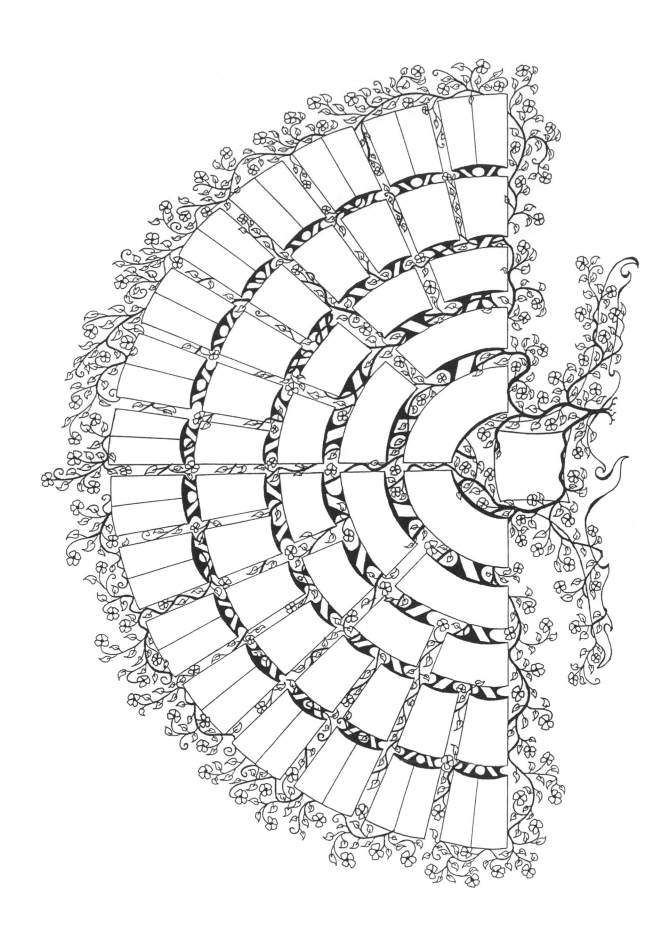

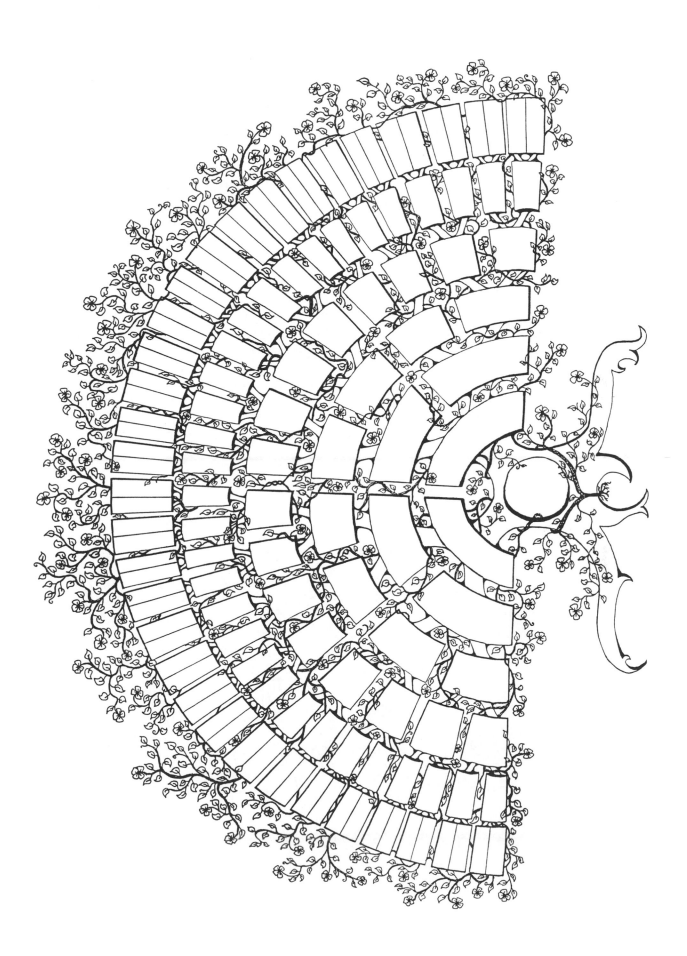

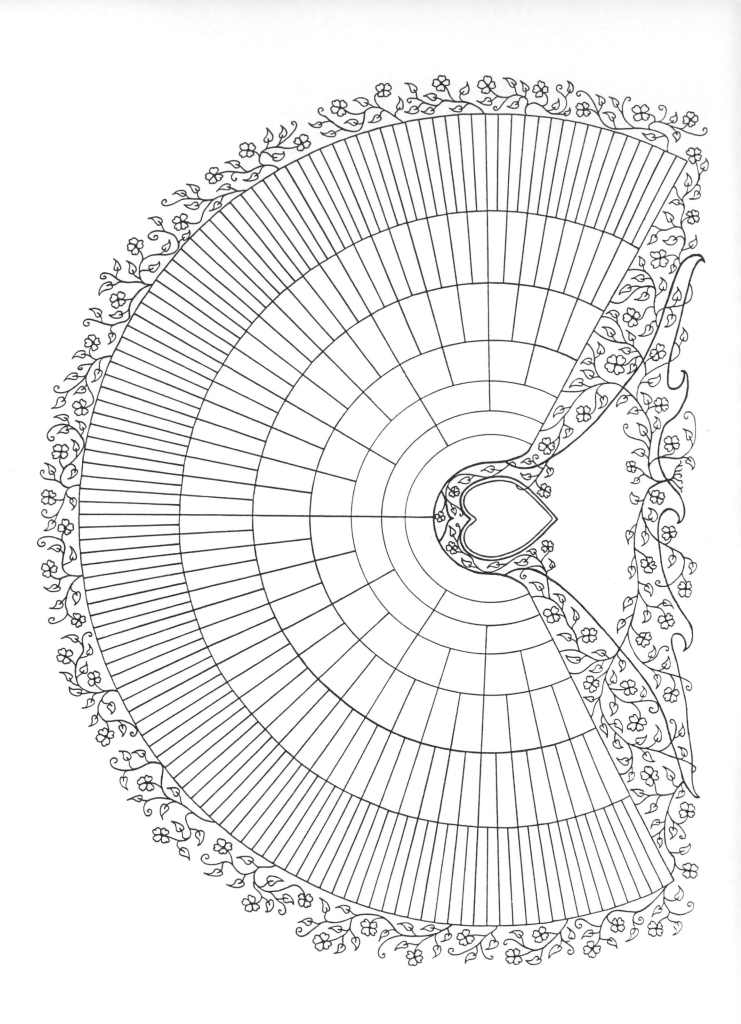

In the palace next to the weeping willow tree, lived a rich Mandarin and his lovely daughter, Koong Shee. The Mandarin had a secretary, Chang, to help him organize his business affairs. Koong Shee and Chang would meet and talk by the orange tree. They fell in love and wished to marry. But Chang was poor, so the Mandarin refused to give his permission for the match. Instead, he arranged for his daughter to marry a wealthy suitor who brought a handsome engagement gift--a box full of jewels and coins. Until the wedding could take place, the Mandarin hid his daughter from Chang by imprisoning Koong Shee in the summer house. But the lovers found ways to communicate. Chang made a small boat out of a coconut shell (complete with sail) which he placed in the river. The tiny boat, with a note from Chang inside, found its way to Koong Shee. In reply, Koong Shee wrote messages on ivory tiles which she placed into the coconut boat--returning the little vessel to the river. They arranged to elope on the night before the wedding. Chang entered the Mandarin's garden, despite the barricades set up to keep him out, and the lovers stole away together. But Koong Shee's father saw them and gave chase. The three were seen running on the bridge--Chang in front with a staff; Koong Shee carrying the box of jewels and coins; and the Mandarin chasing them with a lantern. The lovers made good their escape by sailing away in a boat which Chang had waiting. They traded the purloined jewels and coins for a house on an isolated island; asked the benevolent Powers to bless their union; and lived happily together. But Koong Shee's rejected suitor, angry over the loss of his bride and his treasure, found them and burned their house down. Chang and Koong Shee perished in the flames. A kindly Power saw and took pity upon the lovers. Out of the ashes arose two white swallows--the spirits of Chang and Koong Shee--Always Together.

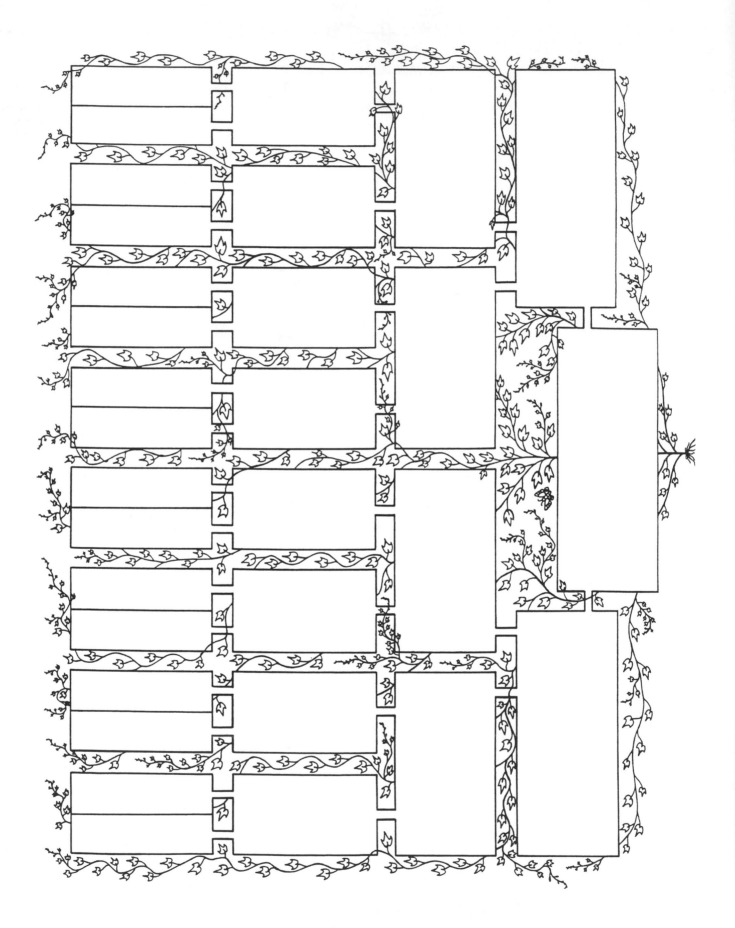

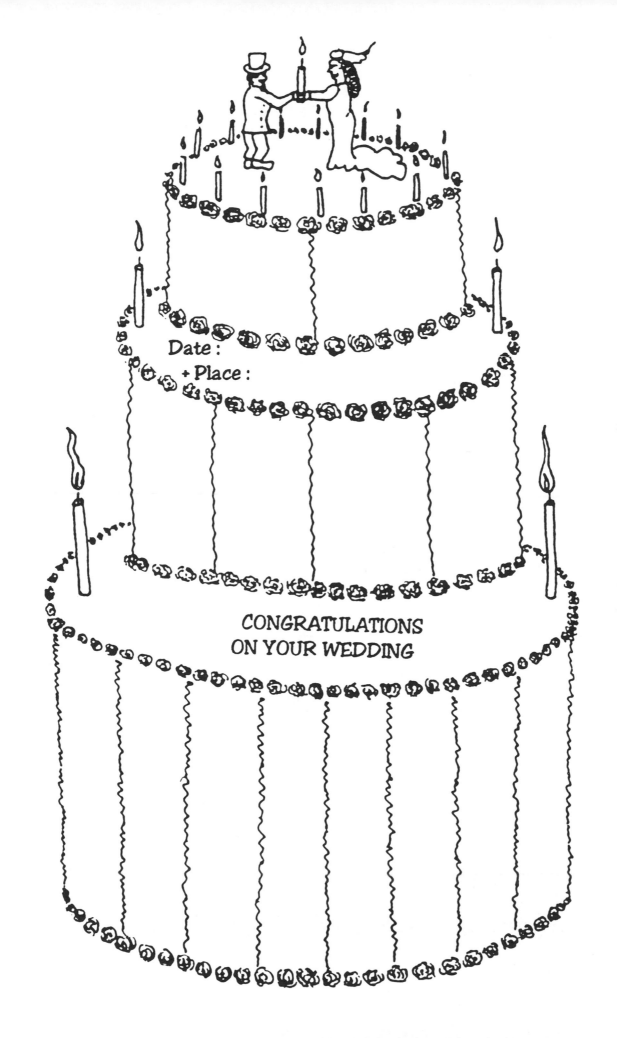

Date :

+ Place :

CONGRATULATIONS
ON YOUR WEDDING

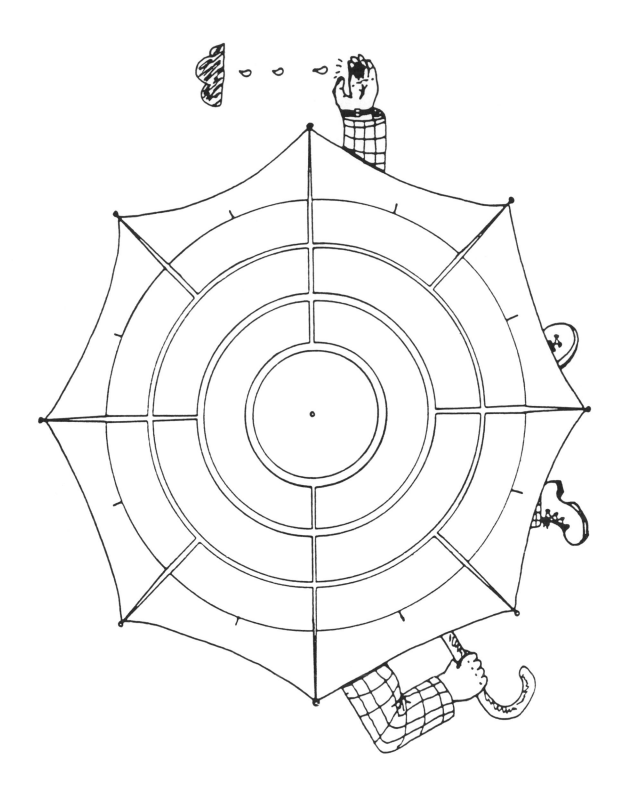

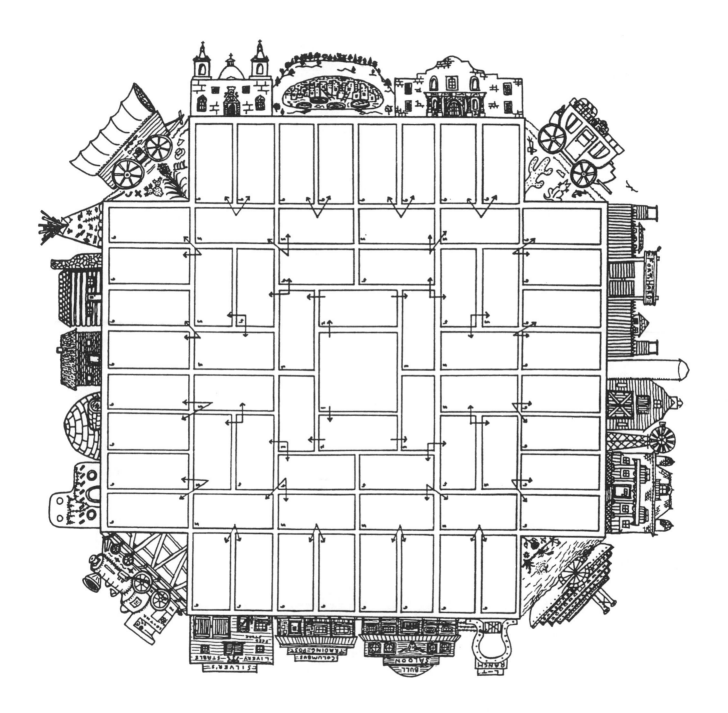

1.		
2.	17.	
3.	18.	
4.	19.	
5.	20.	
6.	21.	
7.	22.	
8.	23.	
9.	24.	
10.	25.	
11.	26.	
12.	27.	
13.	28.	
14.	29.	
15.	30.	
16.	31.	

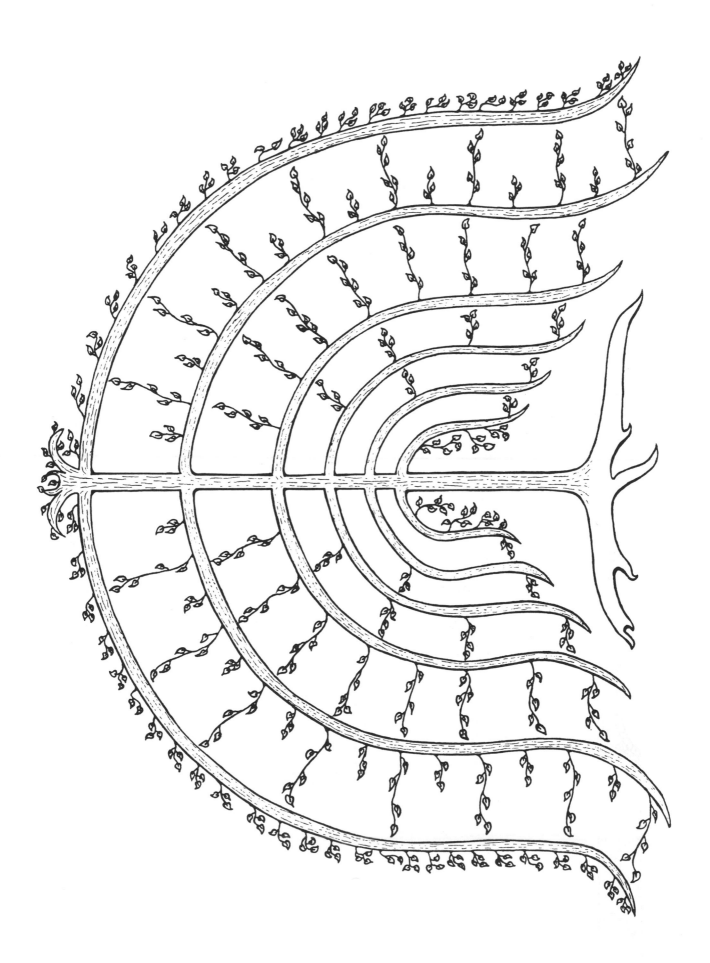

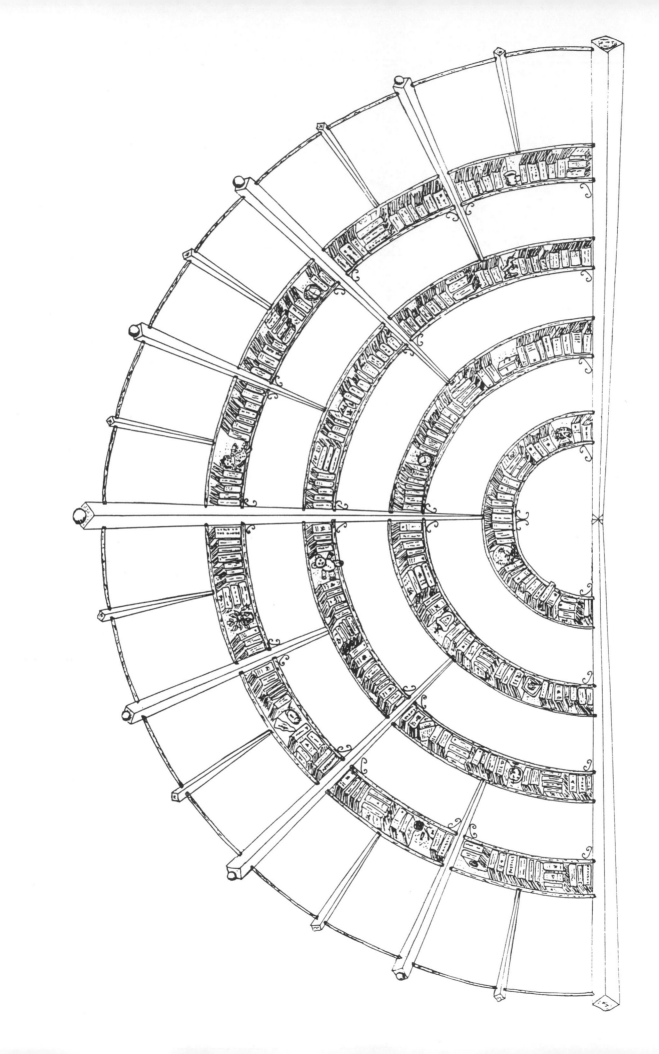

1.

2.	17.
3.	18.
4.	19.
5.	20.
6.	21.
7.	22.
8.	23.
9.	24.
10.	25.
11.	26.
12.	27.
13.	28.
14.	29.
15.	30.
16.	31.

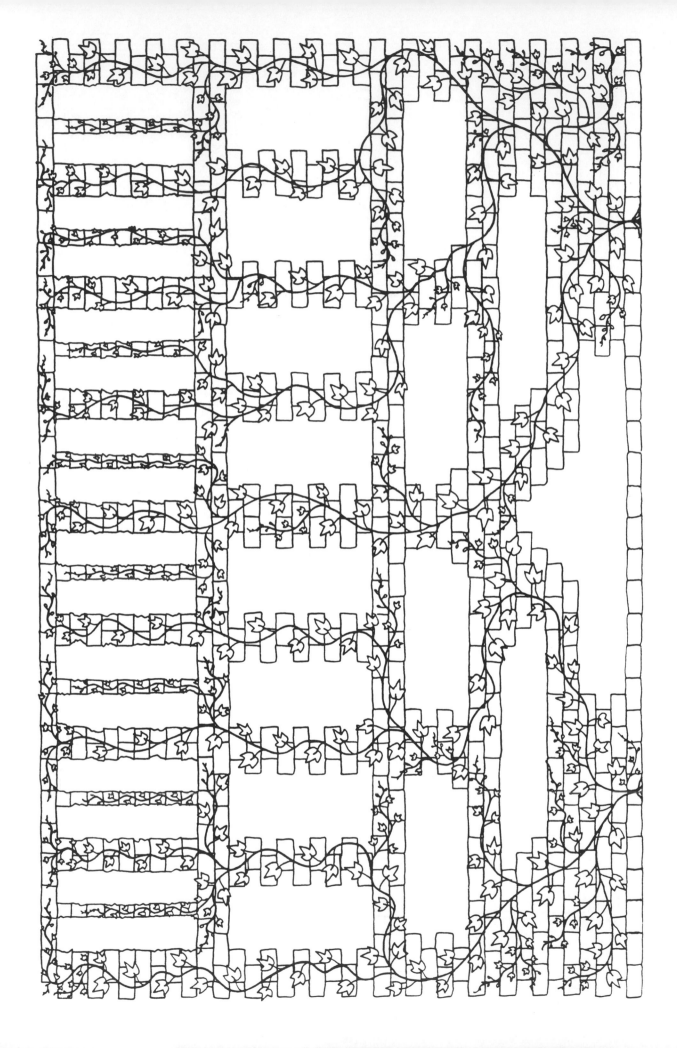

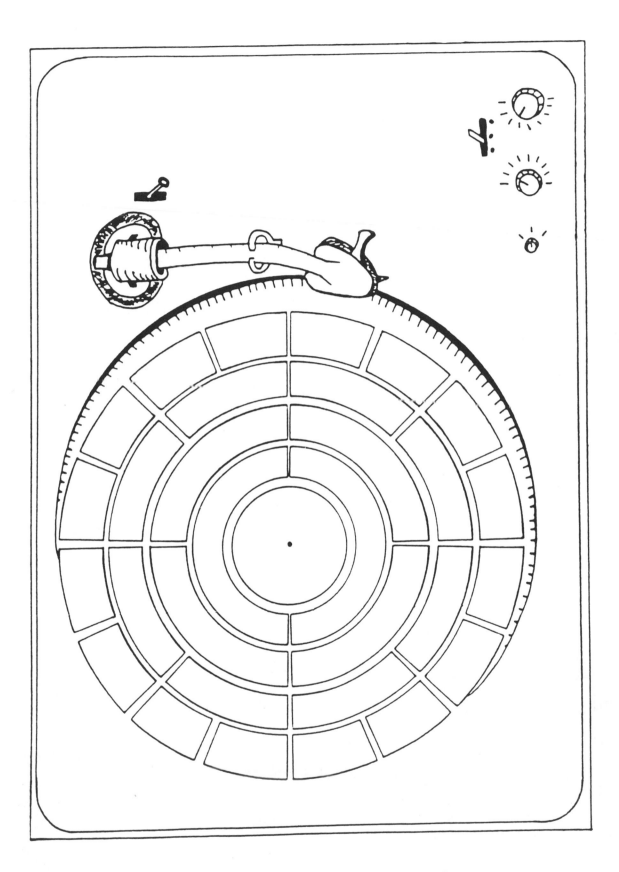

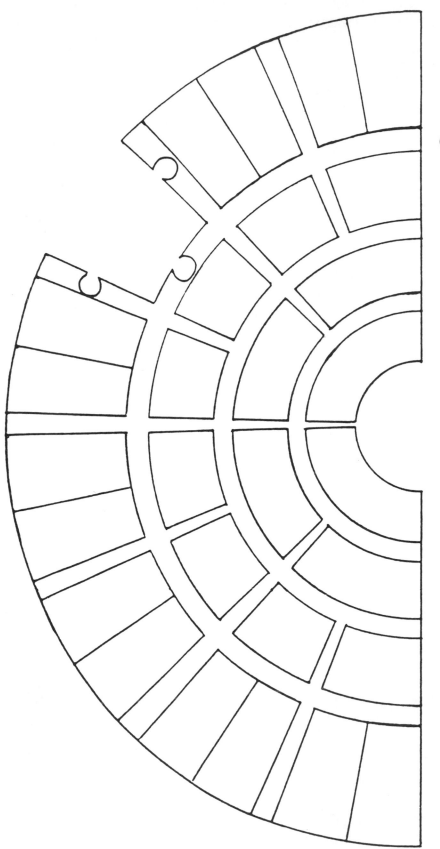

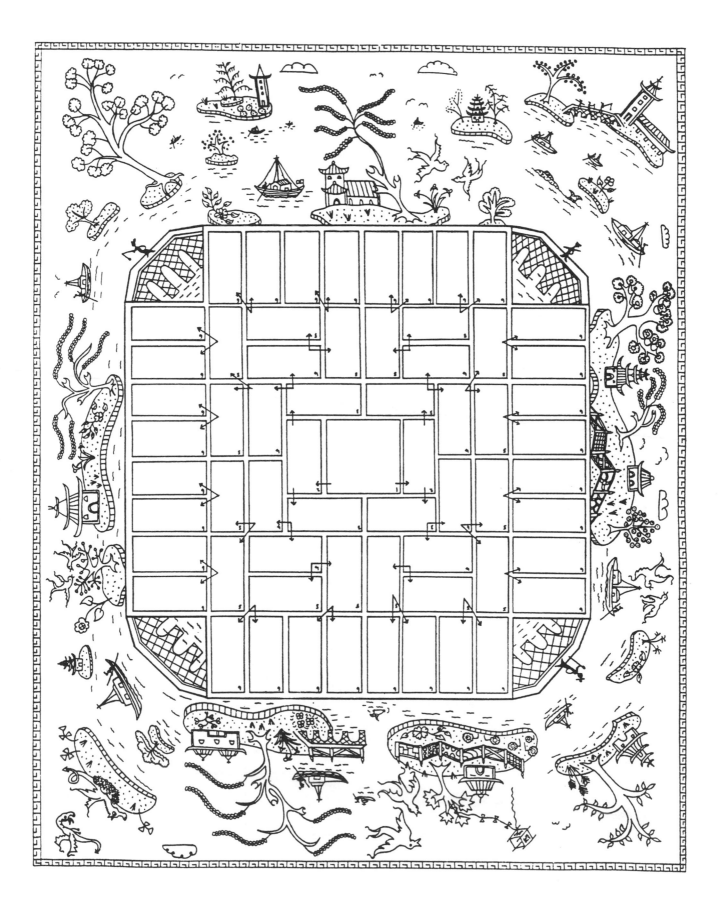

1.	
2.	17.
3.	18.
4.	19.
5.	20.
6.	21.
7.	22.
8.	23.
9.	24.
10.	25.
11.	26.
12.	27.
13.	28.
14.	29.
15.	30.
16.	31.

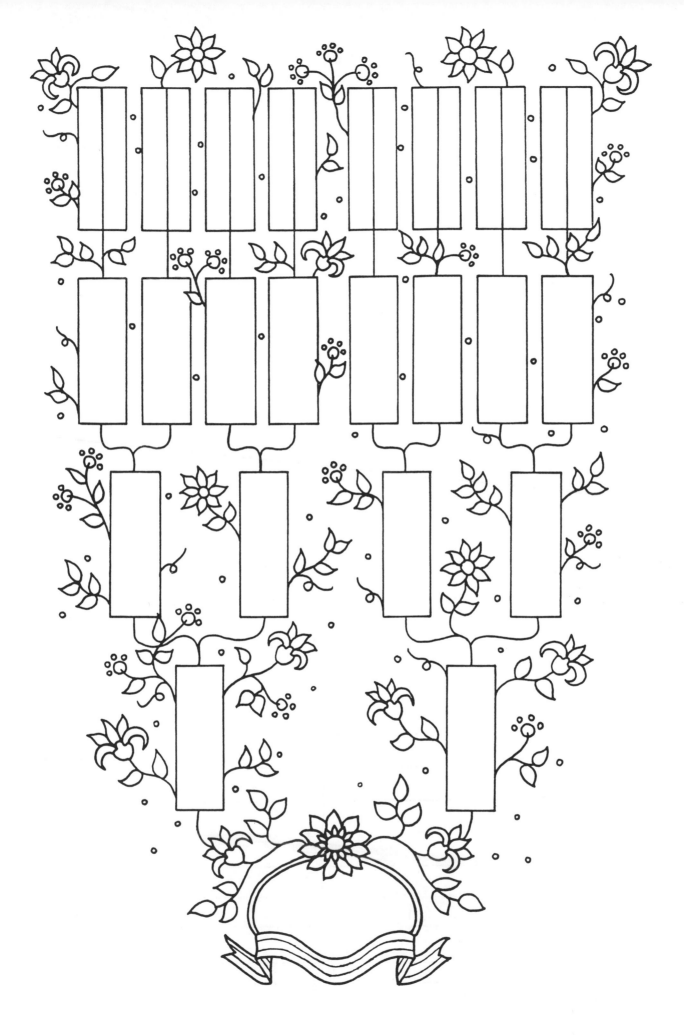

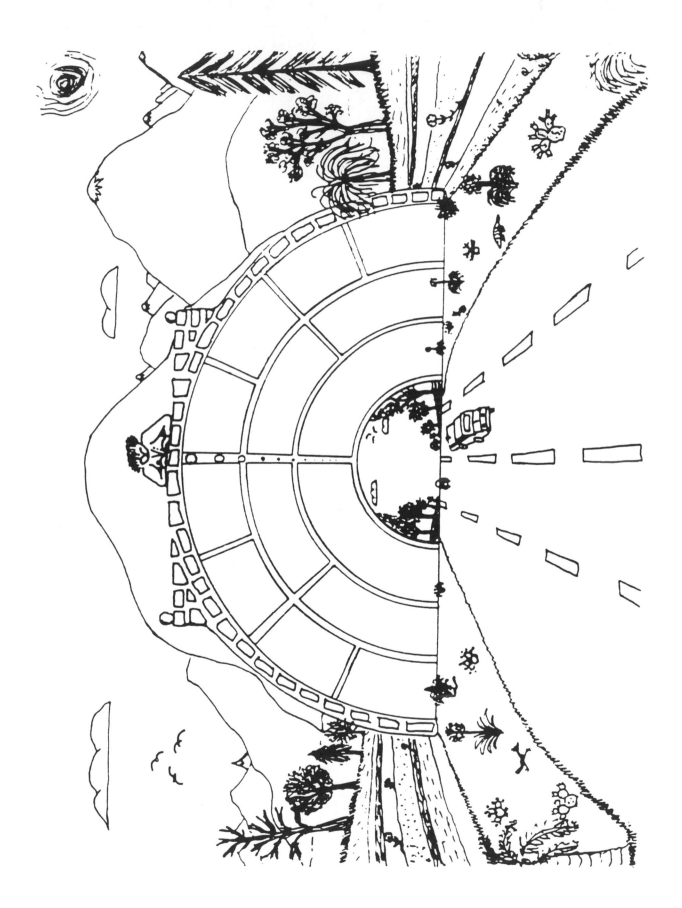

1.

2.   17.

3.   18.

4.   19.

5.   20.

6.   21.

7.   22.

8.   23.

9.   24.

10.   25.

11.   26.

12.   27.

13.   28.

14.   29.

15.   30.

16.   31.

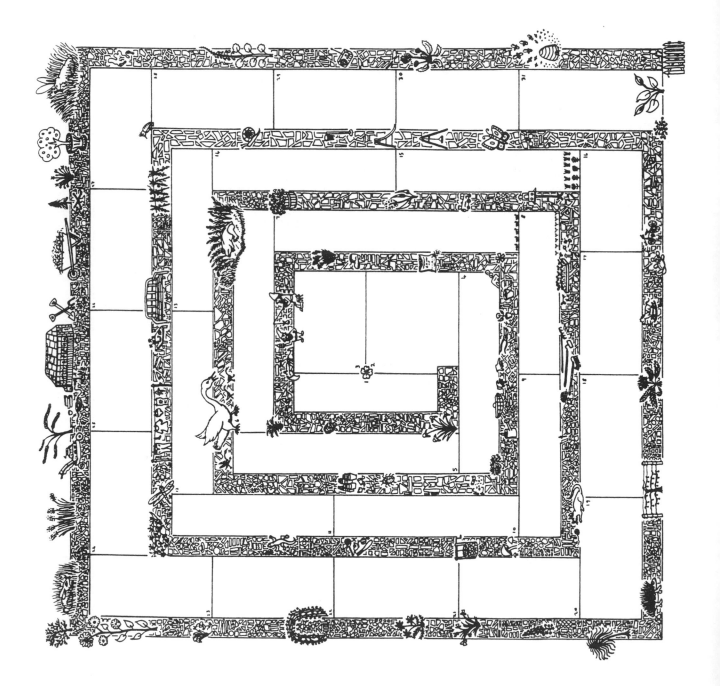

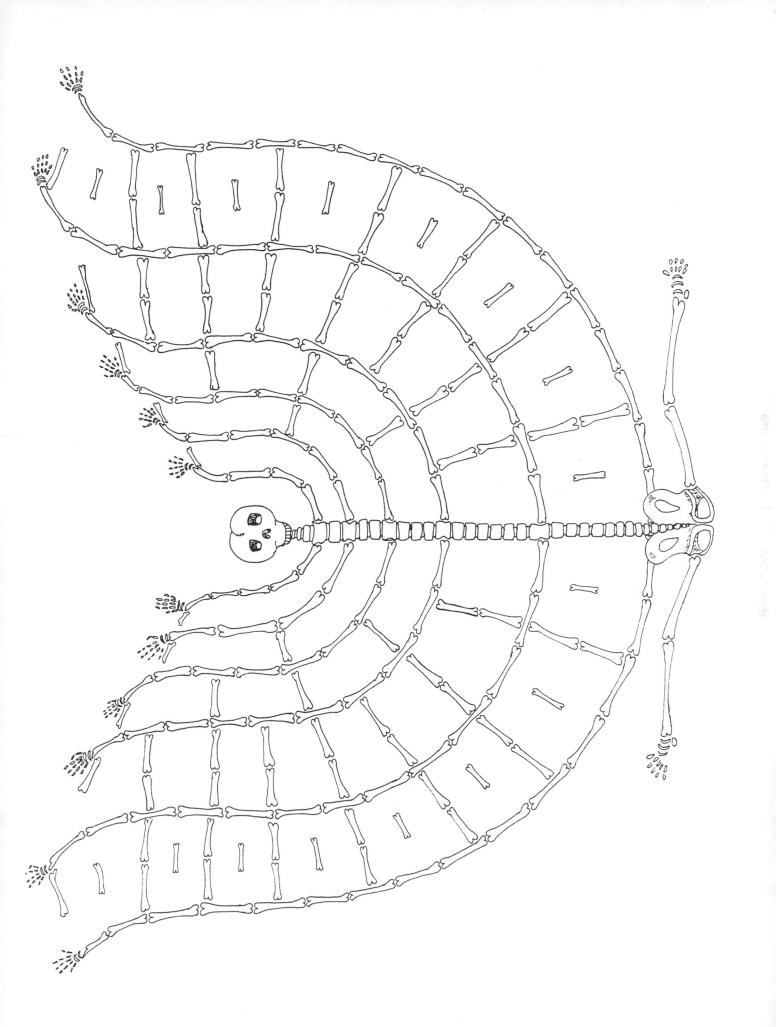

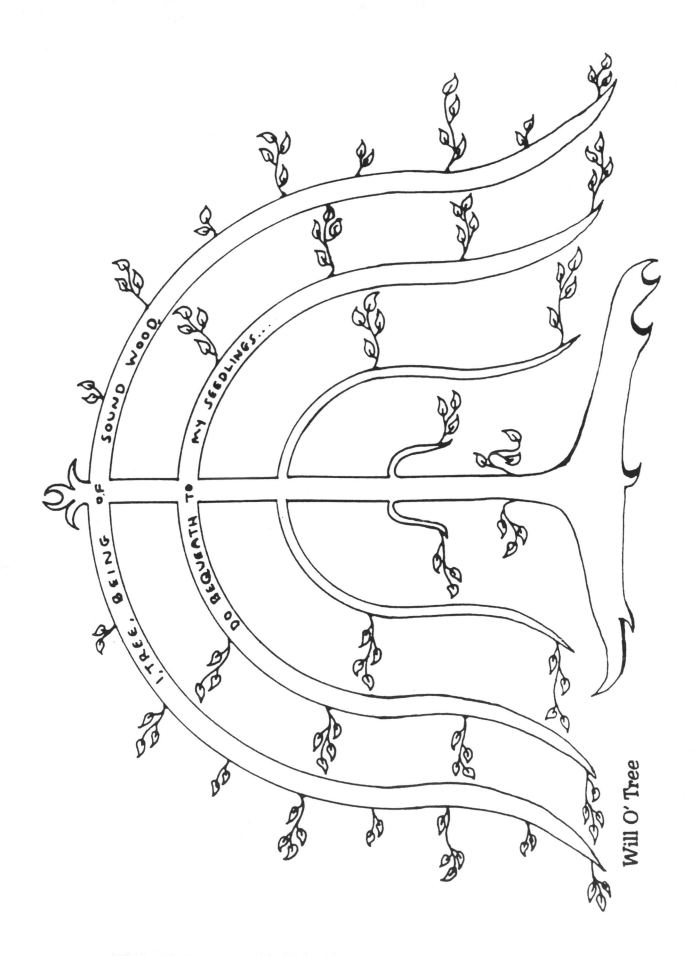

I, TREE, BEING OF SOUND WOOD, DO BEQUEATH TO MY SEEDLINGS...

Will O' Tree

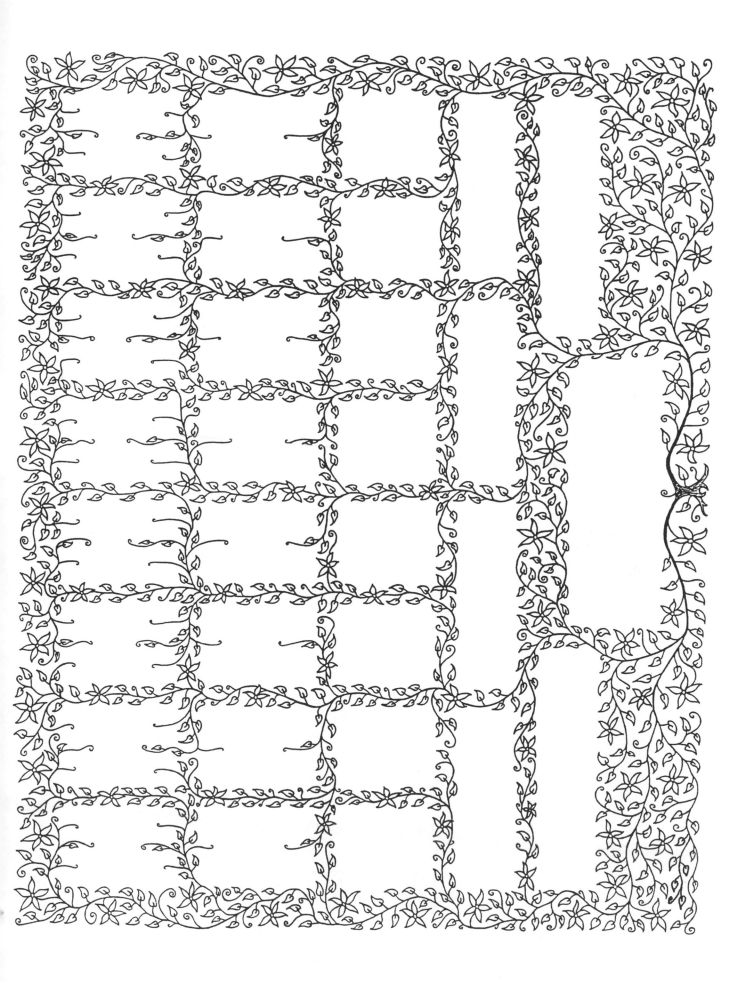

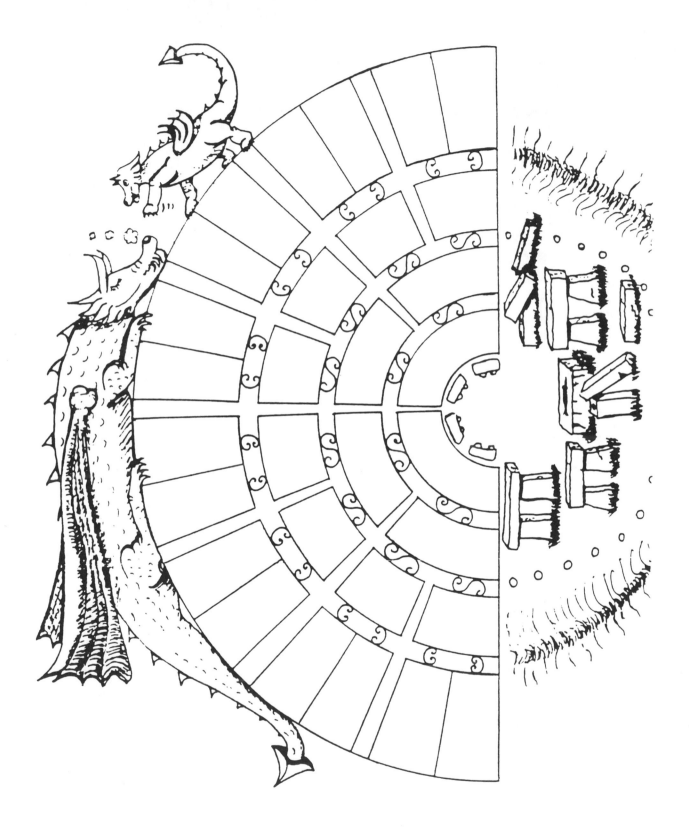

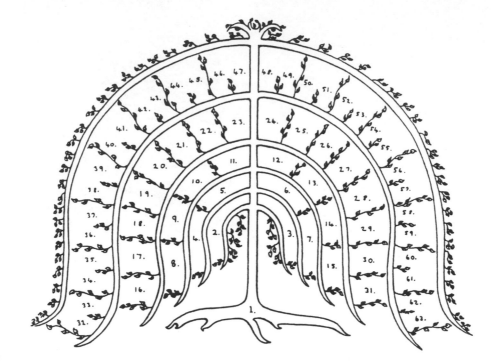

1. _____

2. _____ 33. _____

3. _____ 34. _____

4. _____ 35. _____

5. _____ 36. _____

6. _____ 37. _____

7. _____ 38. _____

8. _____ 39. _____

9. _____ 40. _____

10. _____ 41. _____

11. _____ 42. _____

12. _____ 43. _____

13. _____ 44. _____

14. _____ 45. _____

15. _____ 46. _____

16. _____ 47. _____

17. _____ 48. _____

18. _____ 49. _____

19. _____ 50. _____

20. _____ 51. _____

21. _____ 52. _____

22. _____ 53. _____

23. _____ 54. _____

24. _____ 55. _____

25. _____ 56. _____

26. _____ 57. _____

27. _____ 58. _____

28. _____ 59. _____

29. _____ 60. _____

30. _____ 61. _____

31. _____ 62. _____

32. _____ 63. _____

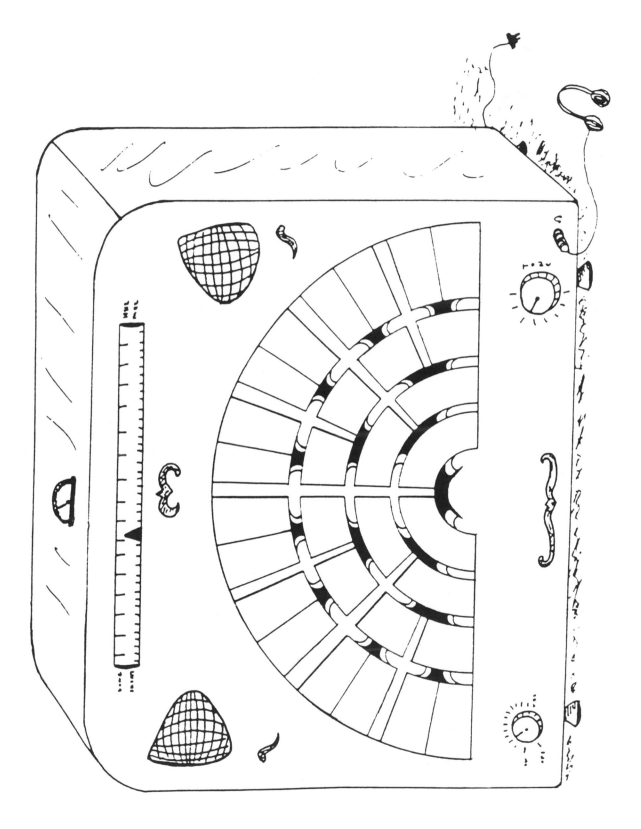

1.	
2.	17.
3.	18.
4.	19.
5.	20.
6.	21.
7.	22.
8.	23.
9.	24.
10.	25.
11.	26.
12.	27.
13.	28.
14.	29.
15.	30.
16.	31.

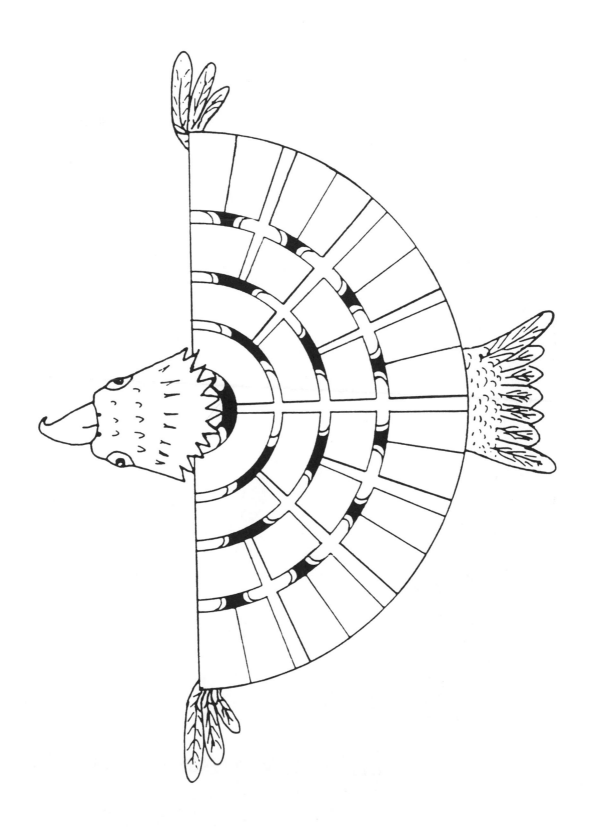

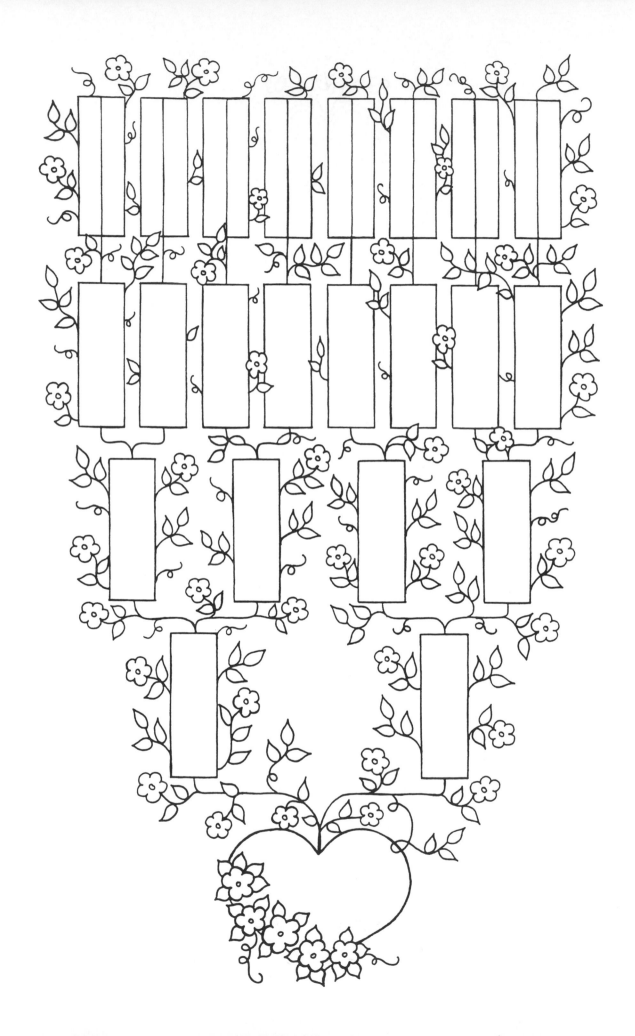

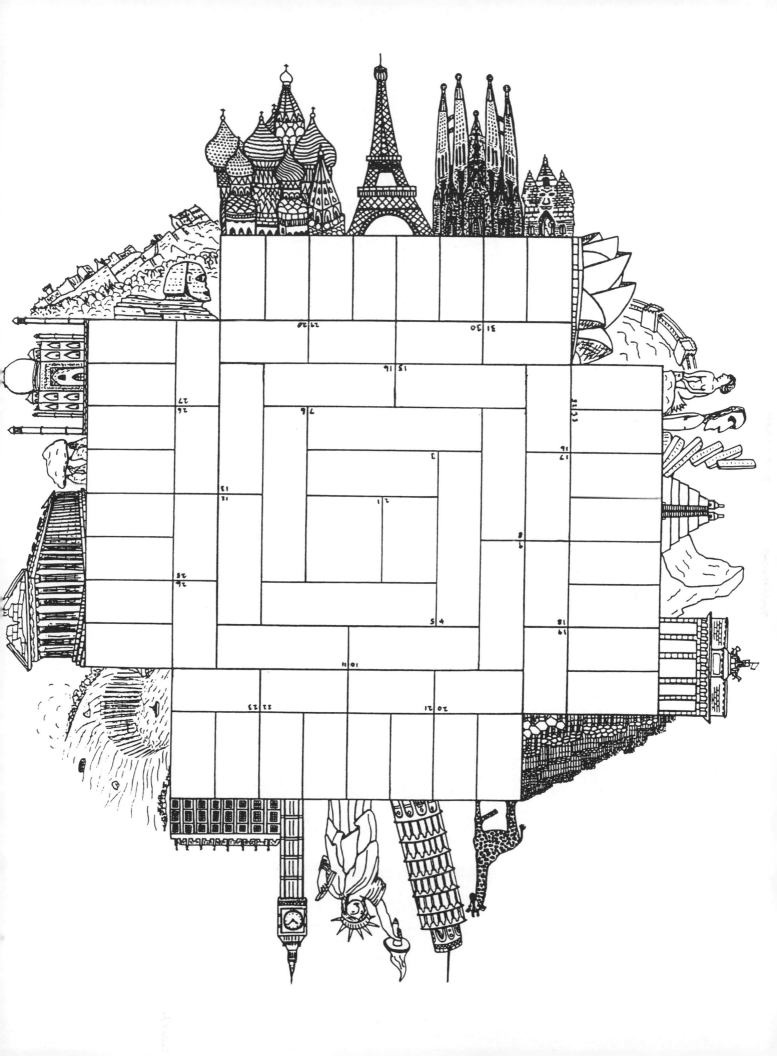

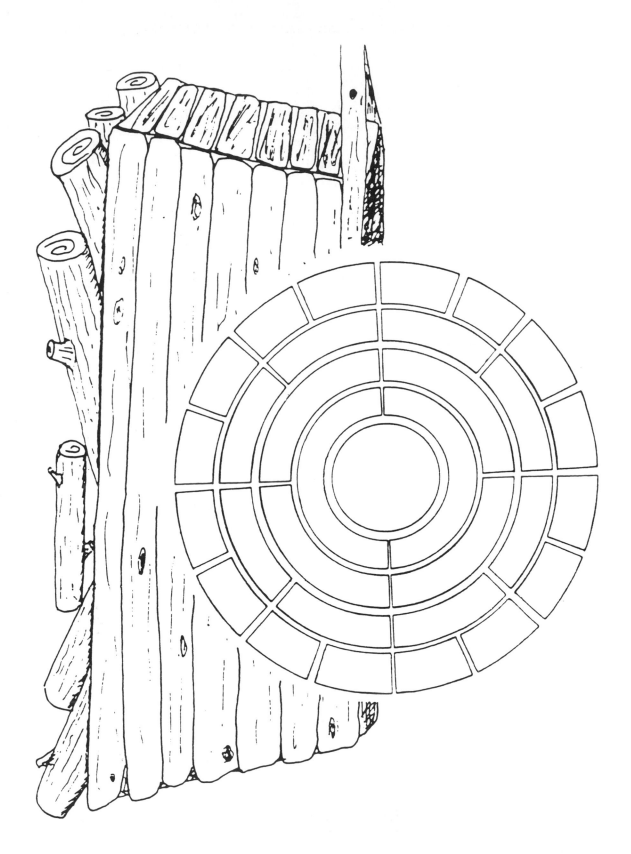

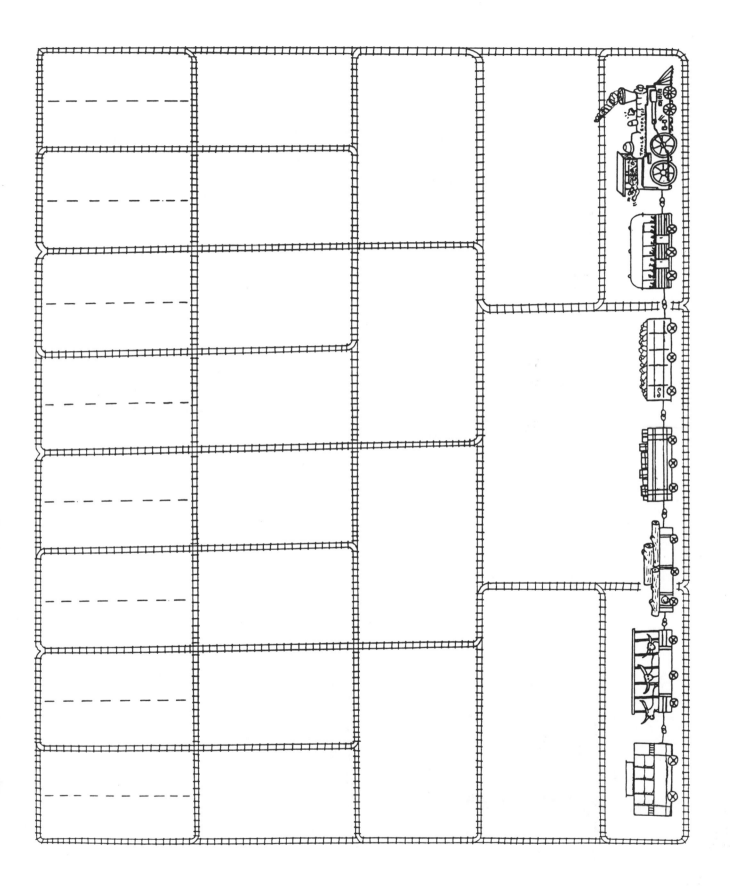

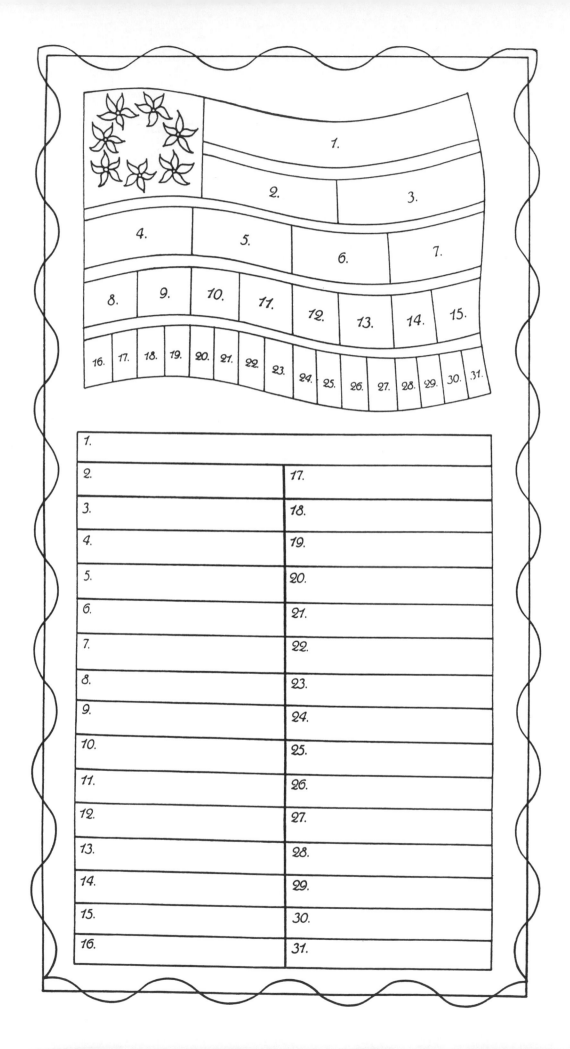

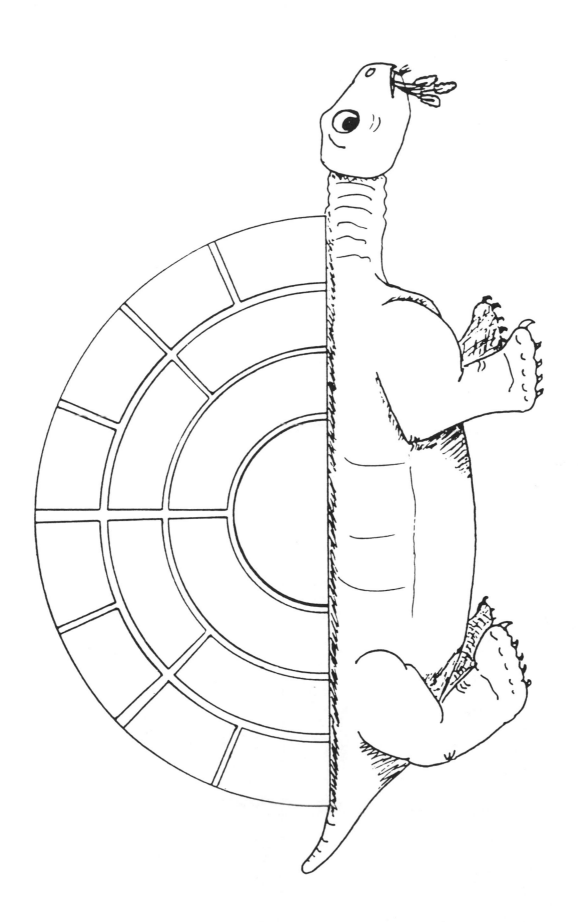

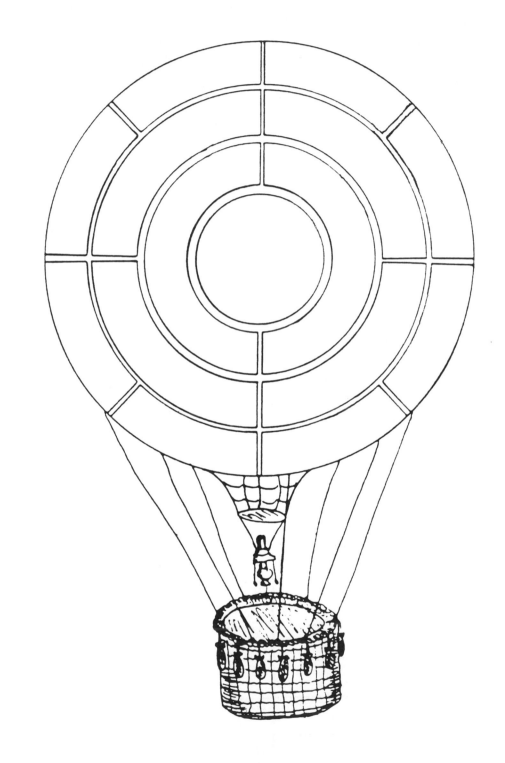

1.	
2.	17.
3.	18.
4.	19.
5.	20.
6.	21.
7.	22.
8.	23.
9.	24.
10.	25.
11.	26.
12.	27.
13.	28.
14.	29.
15.	30.
16.	31.

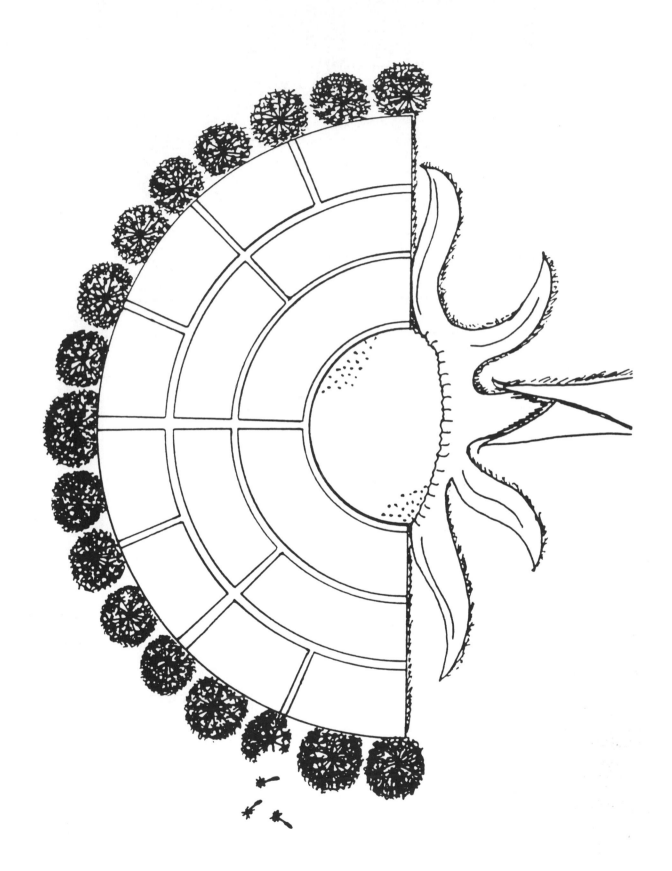

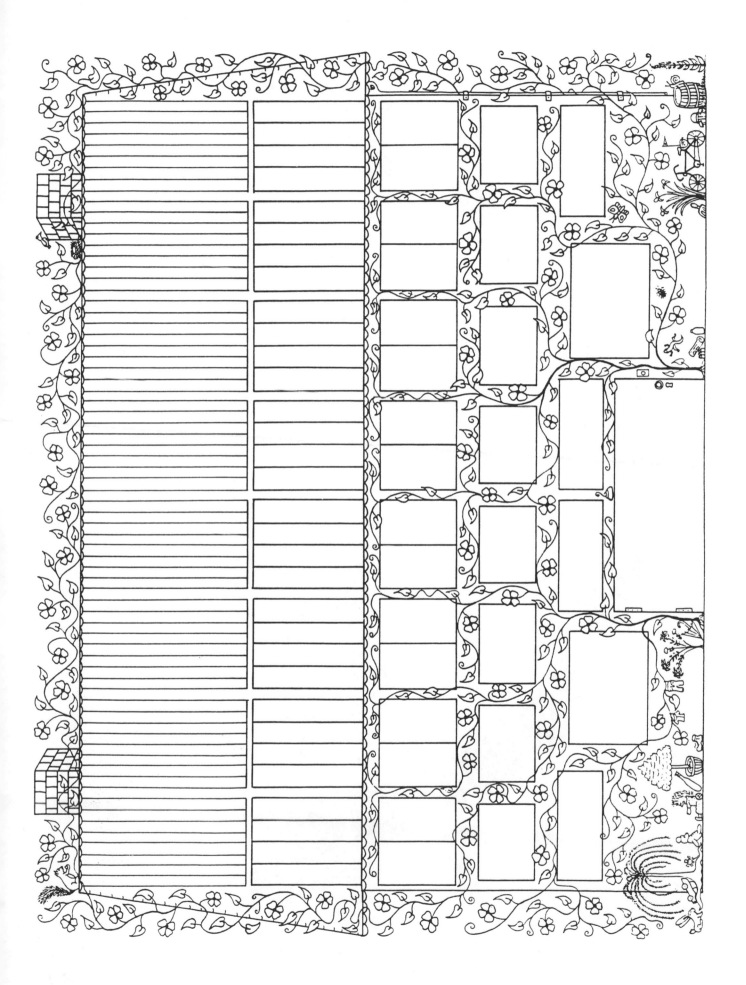

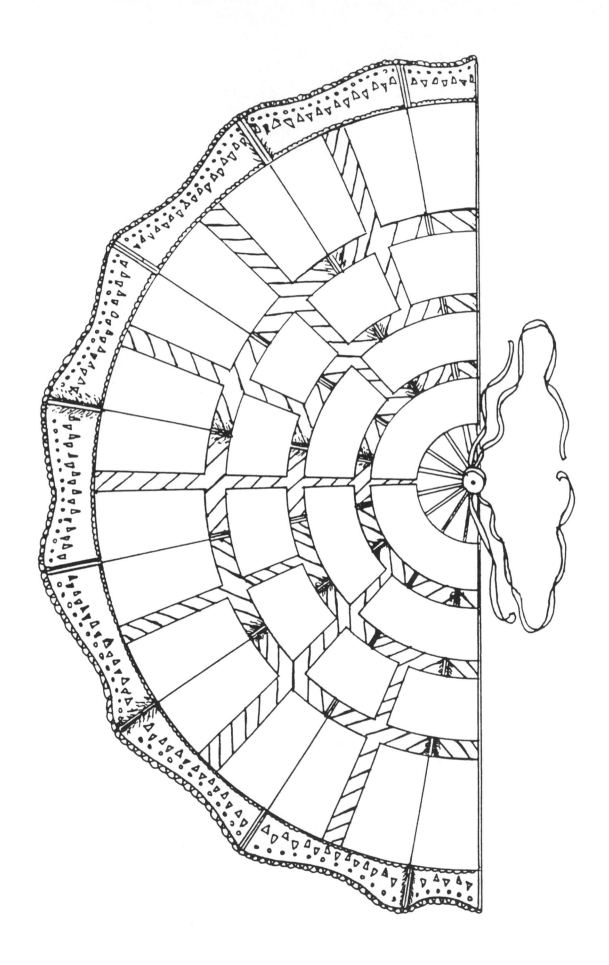

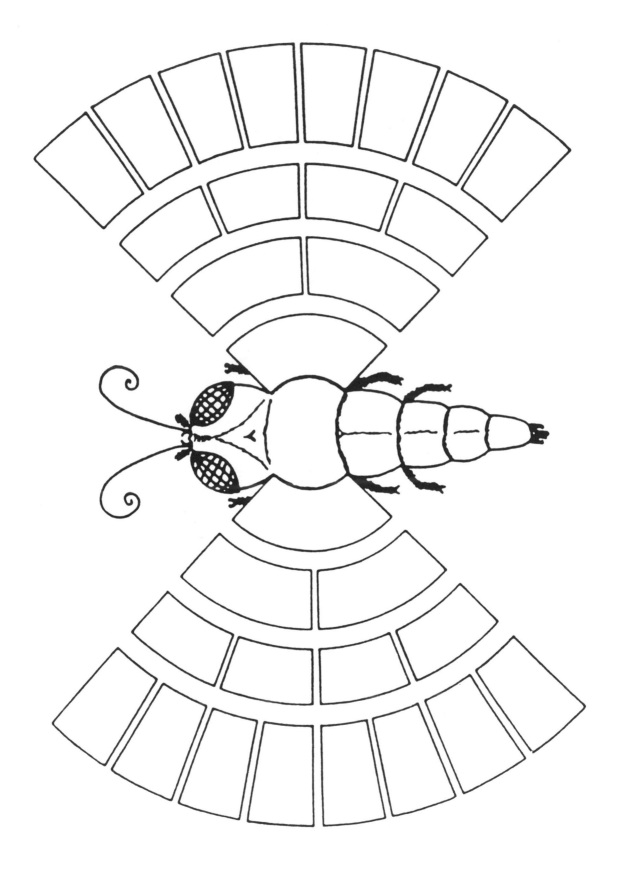

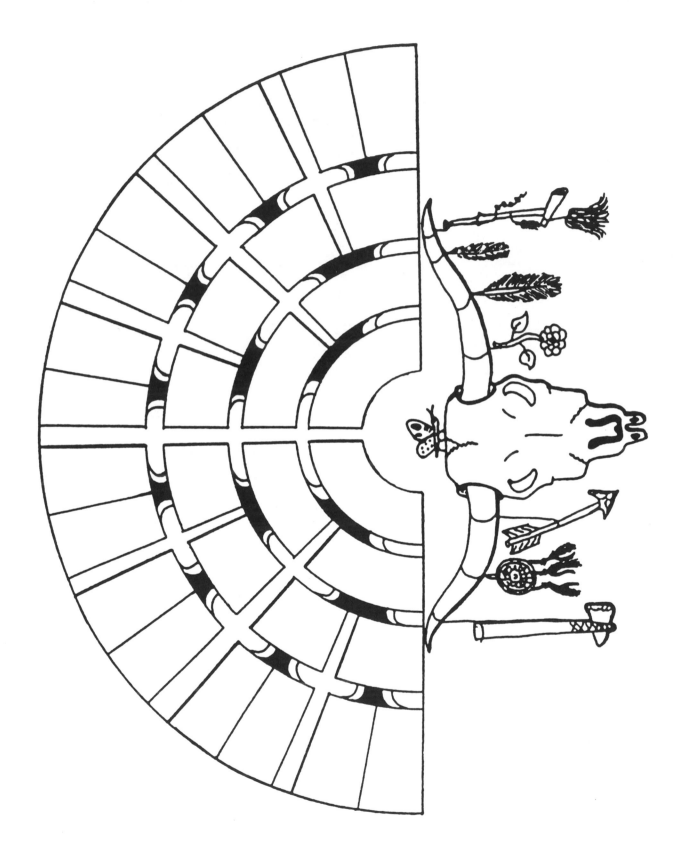

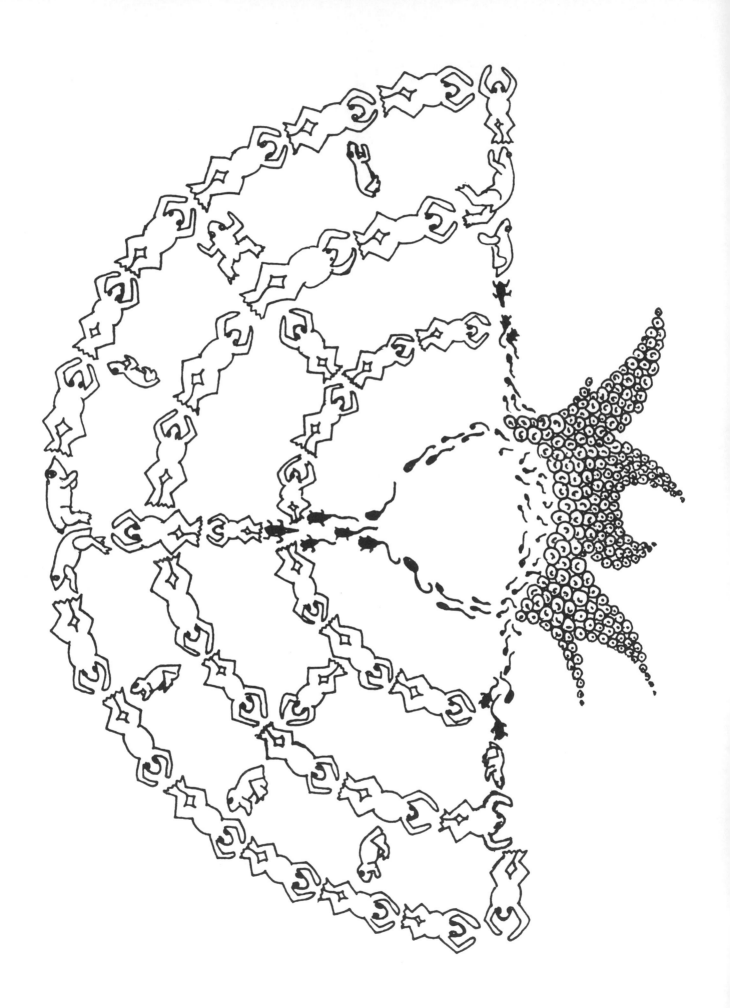

1.		
2.	17.	
3.	18.	
4.	19.	
5.	20.	
6.	21.	
7.	22.	
8.	23.	
9.	24.	
10.	25.	
11.	26.	
12.	27.	
13.	28.	
14.	29.	
15.	30.	
16.	31.	

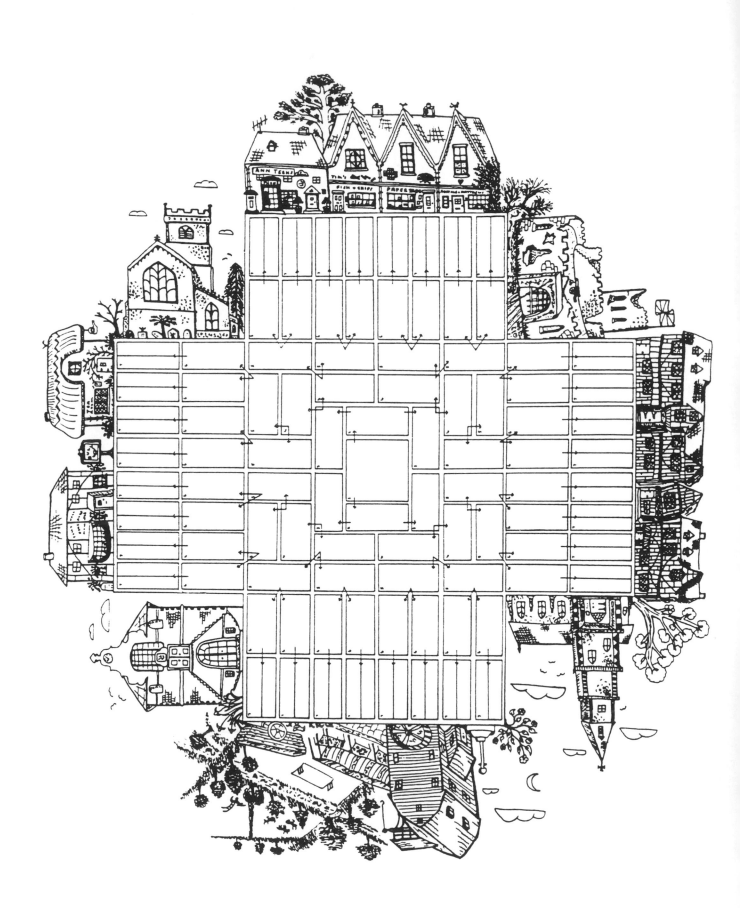

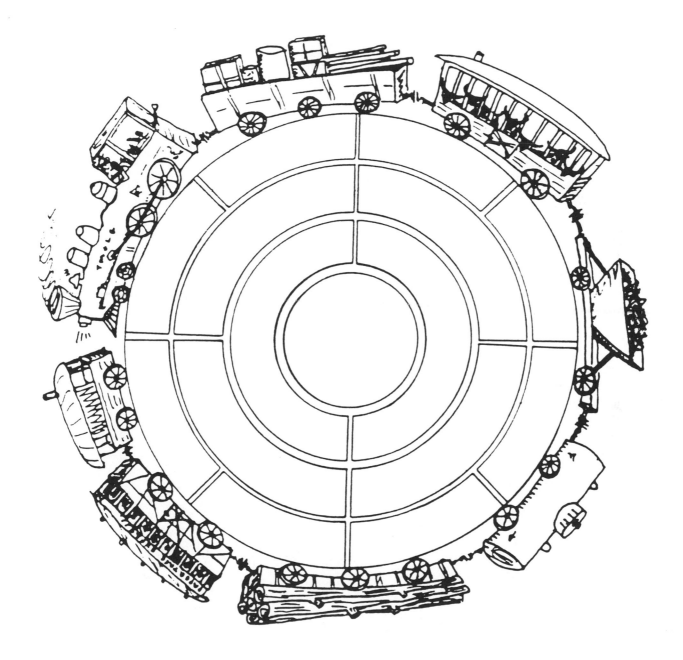

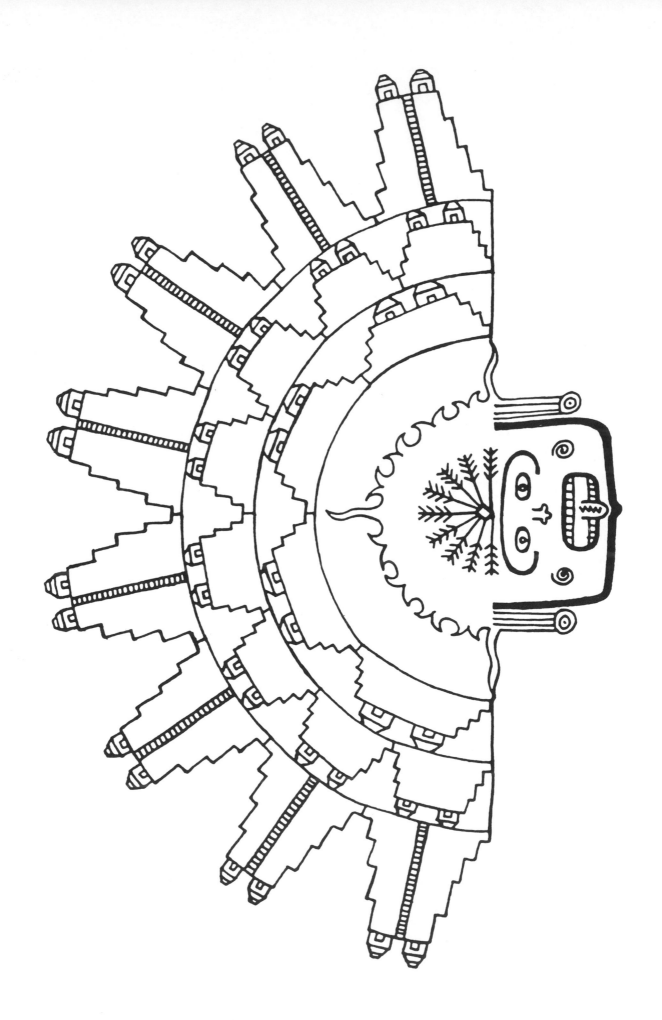

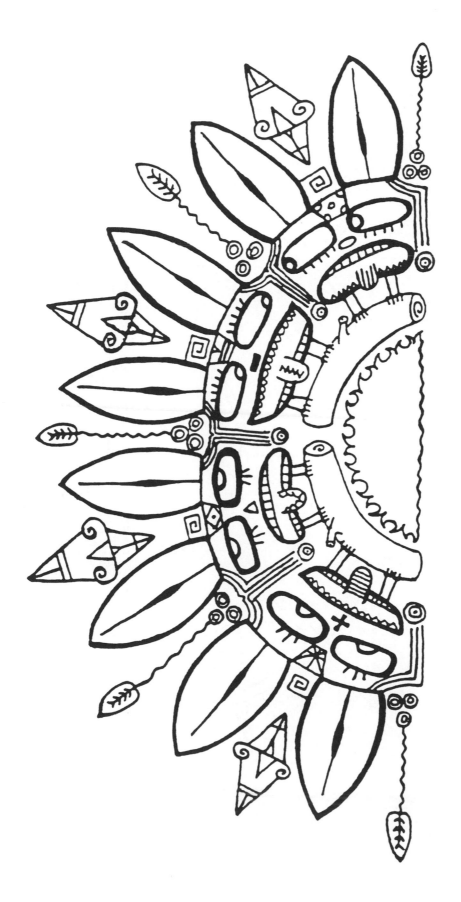

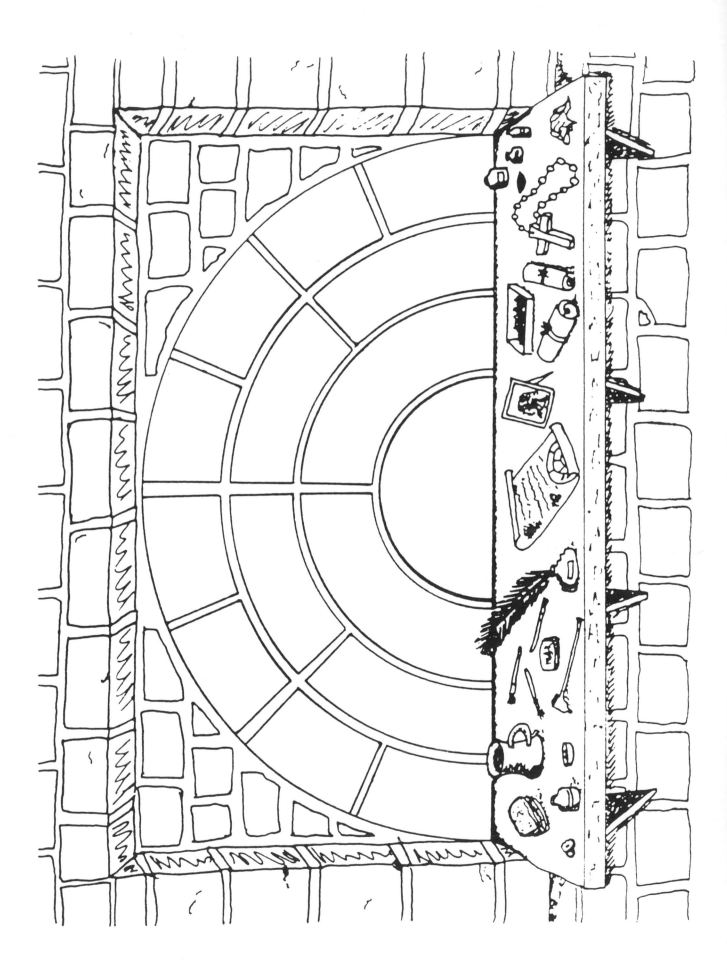

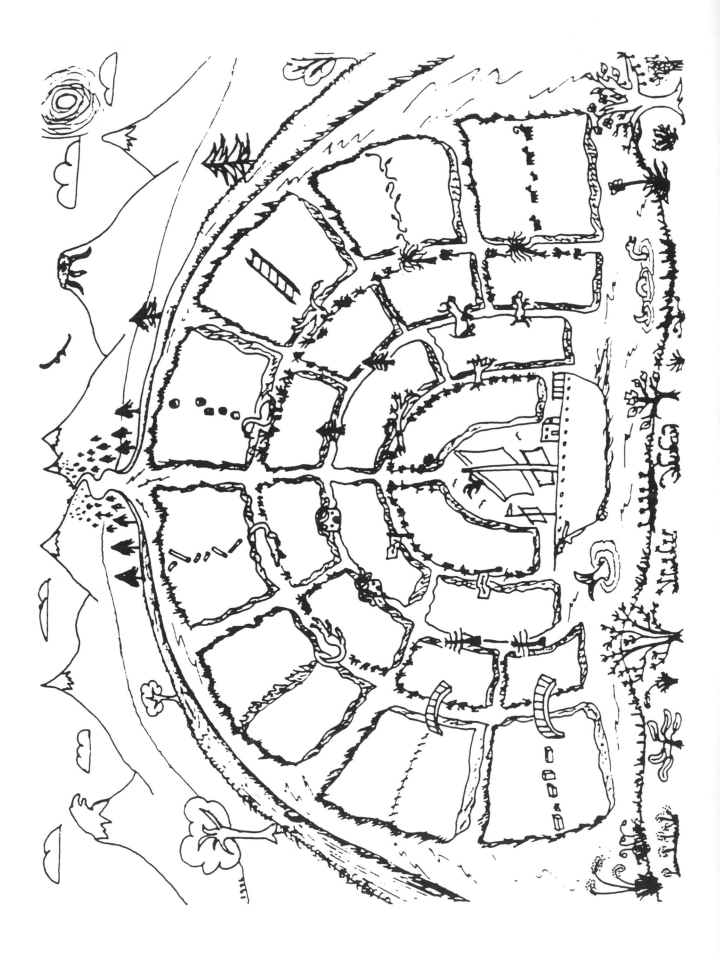

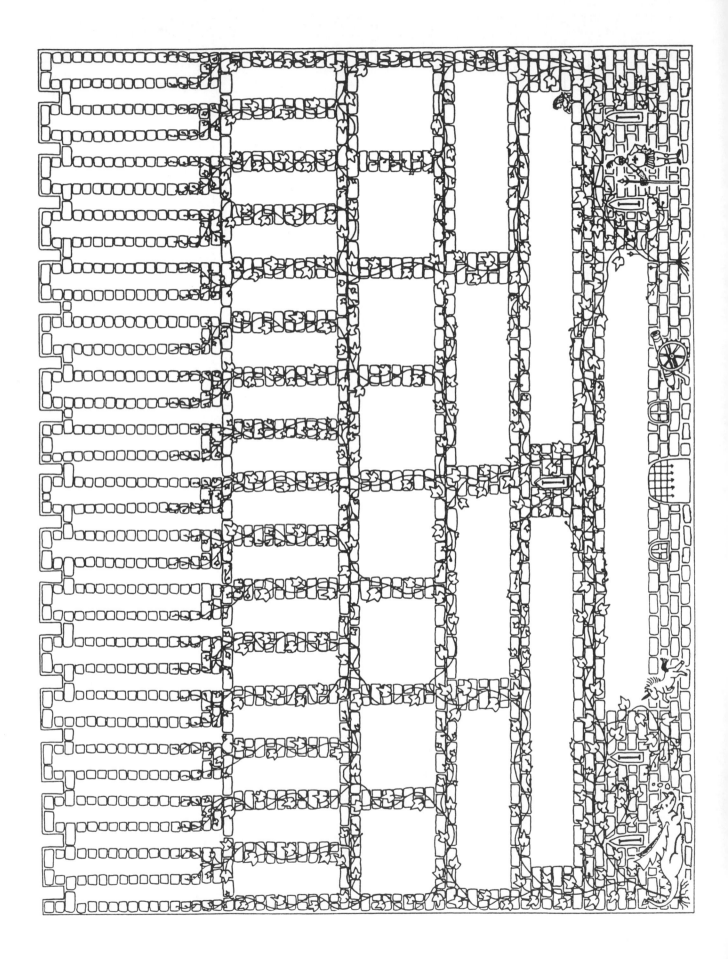

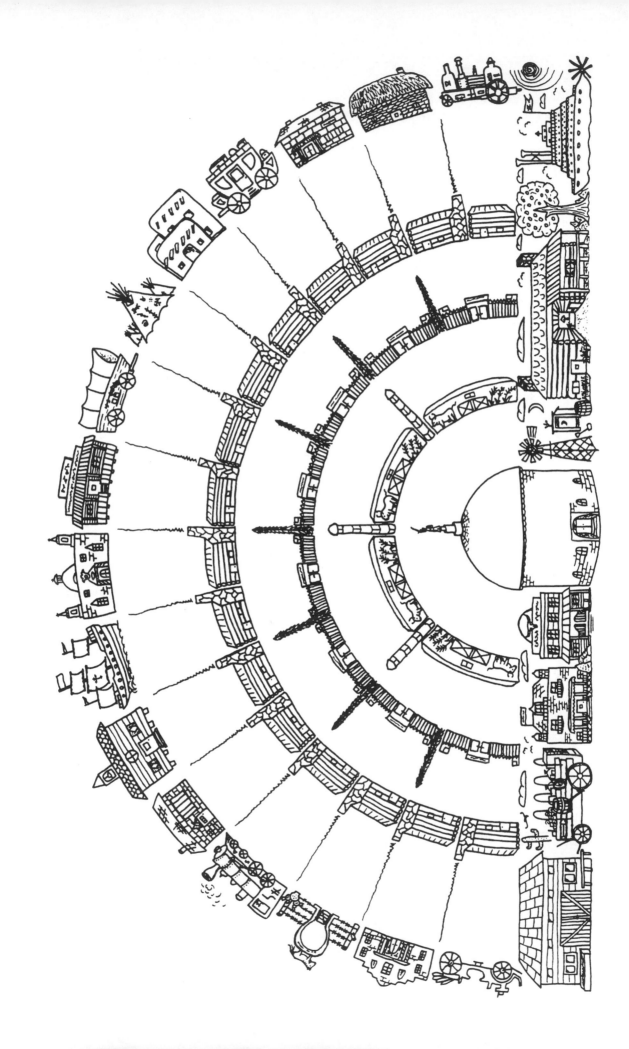

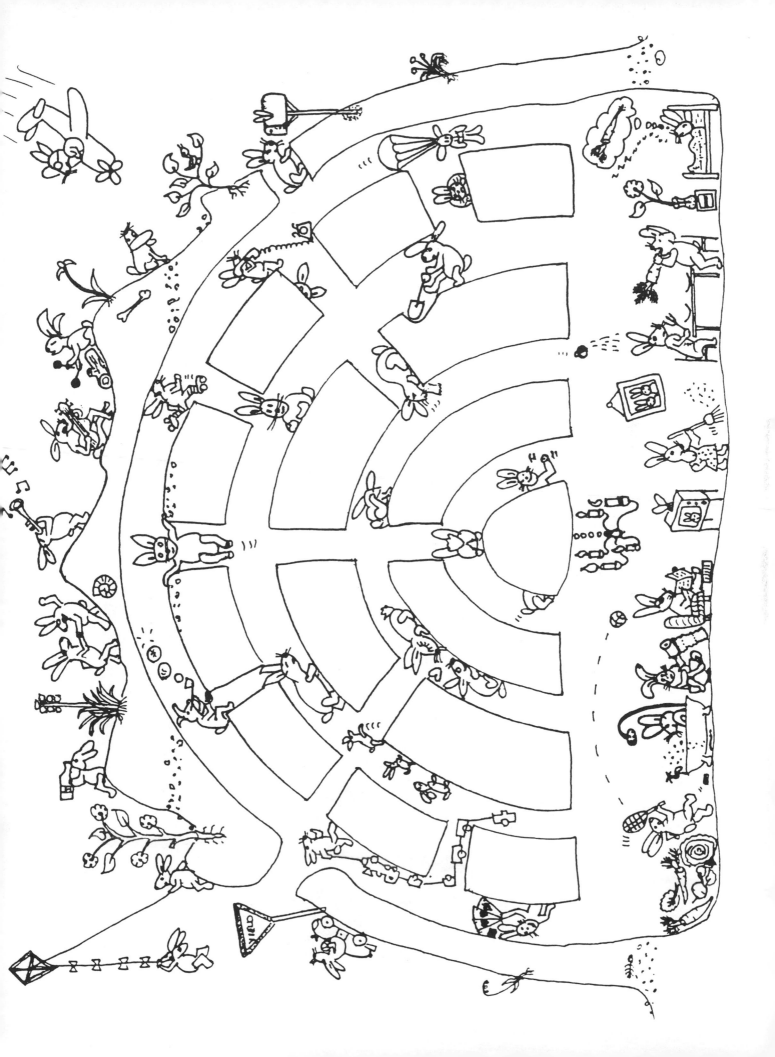

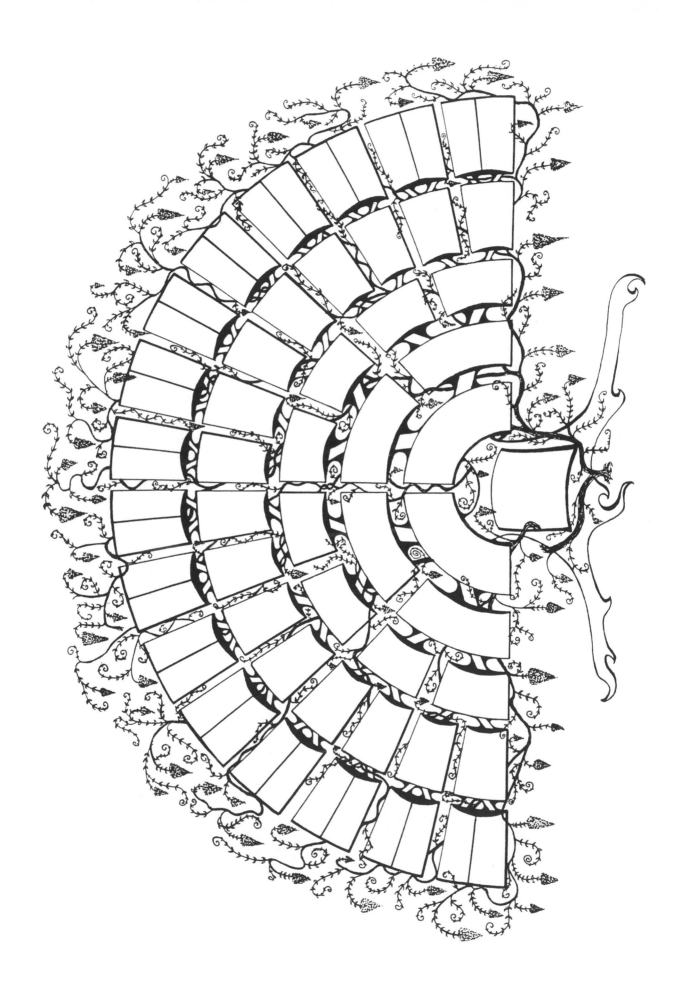

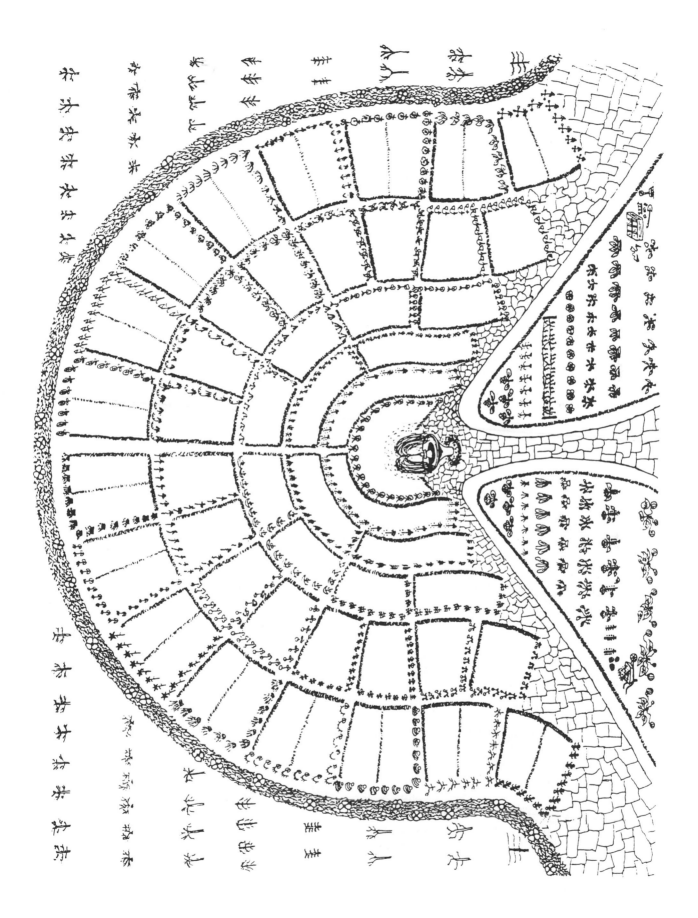

16 17 18 19 20 21 22 23 24 25 26 27 28 29 30 31

8 9 10 11 12 13 14 15

4 5 6 7

2 3

1

Remember

1. _____
2. _____
3. _____
4. _____
5. _____
6. _____
7. _____
8. _____
9. _____
10. _____
11. _____
12. _____
13. _____
14. _____
15. _____
16. _____
17. _____
18. _____
19. _____
20. _____
21. _____
22. _____
23. _____
24. _____
25. _____
26. _____
27. _____
28. _____
29. _____
30. _____
31. _____

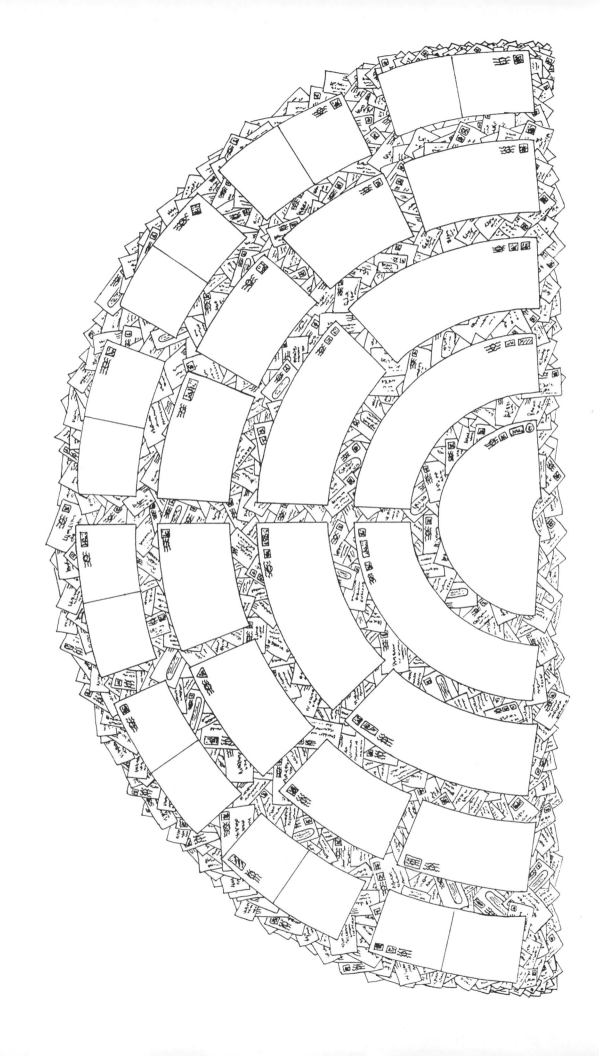

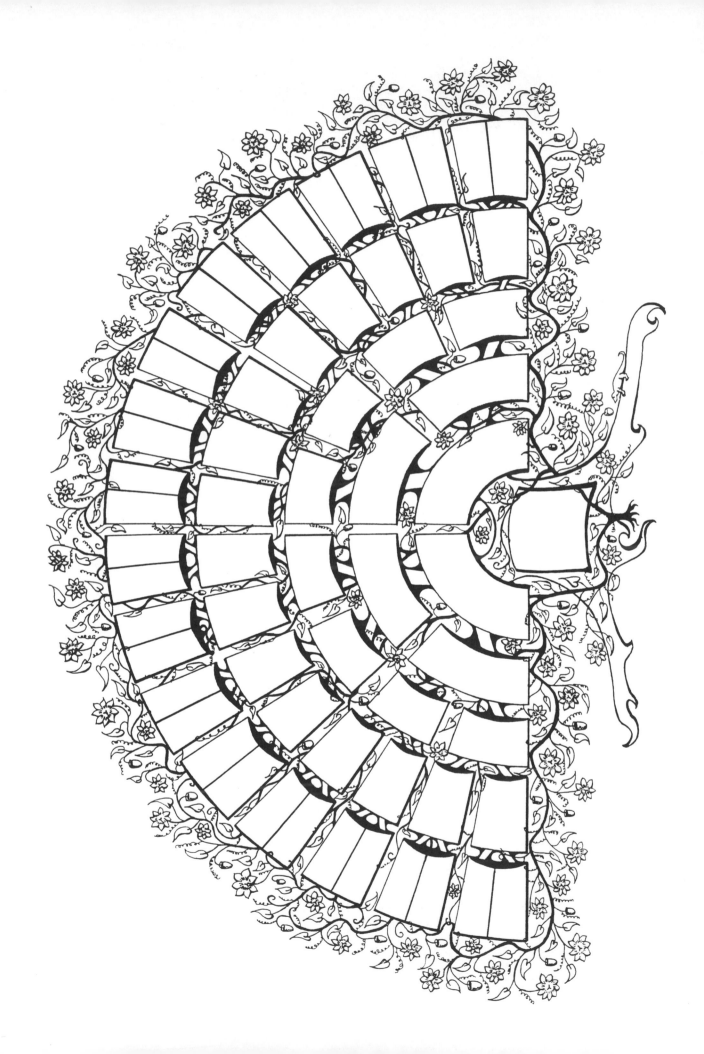

16.	17.	18.	19.	20.	21.	22.	23.	24.	25.	26.	27.	28.	29.	30.	31.

8.	9.	10.	11.	12.	13.	14.	15.

4.	5.	6.	7.

2.	1.	3.

1.	
2.	17.
3.	18.
4.	19.
5.	20.
6.	21.
7.	22.
8.	23.
9.	24.
10.	25.
11.	26.
12.	27.
13.	28.
14.	29.
15.	30.
16.	31.

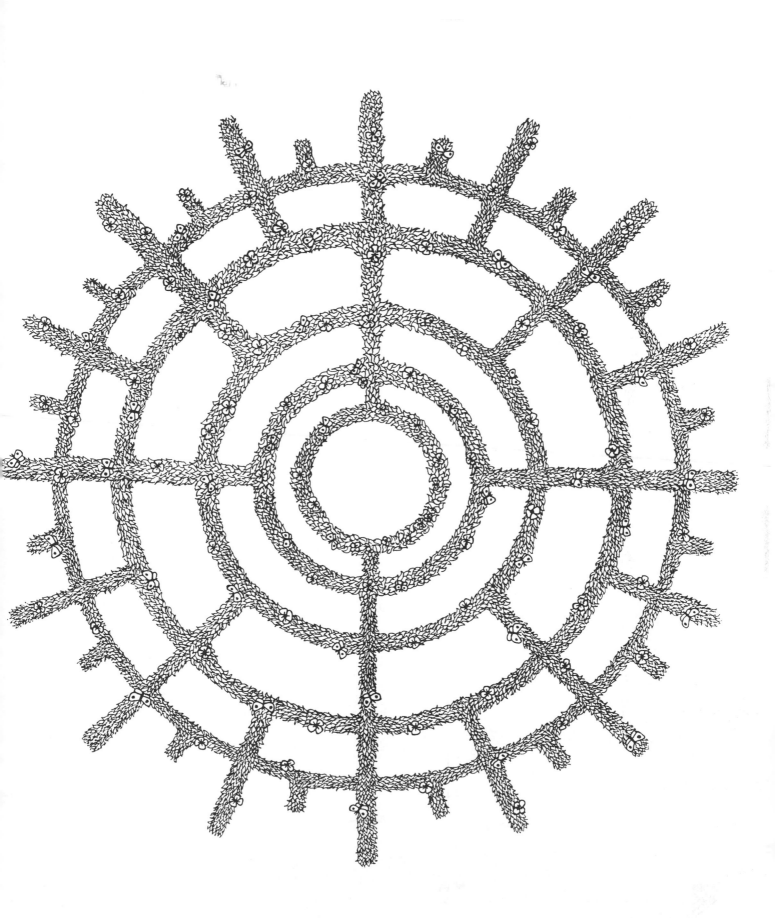

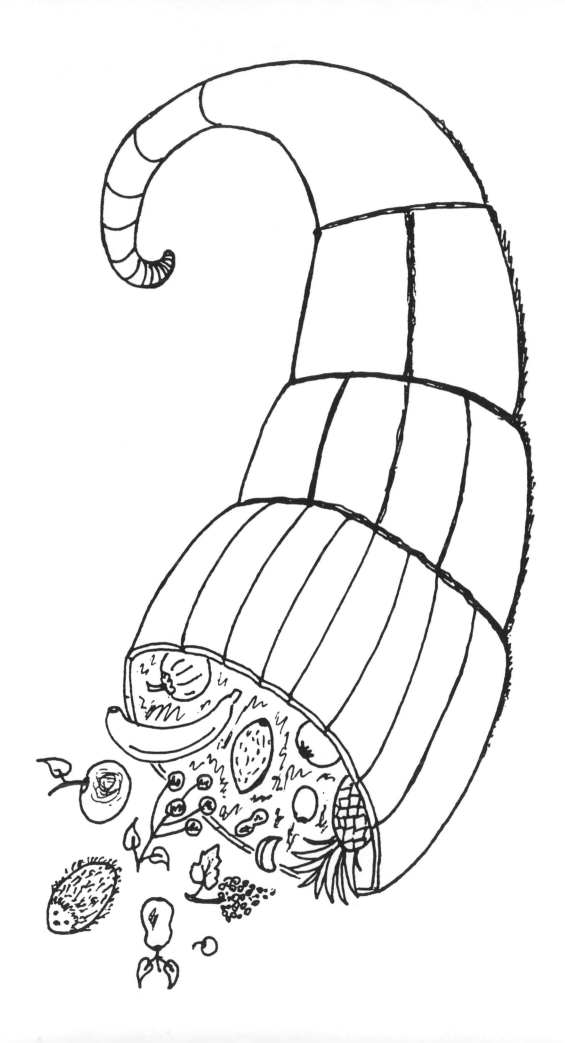

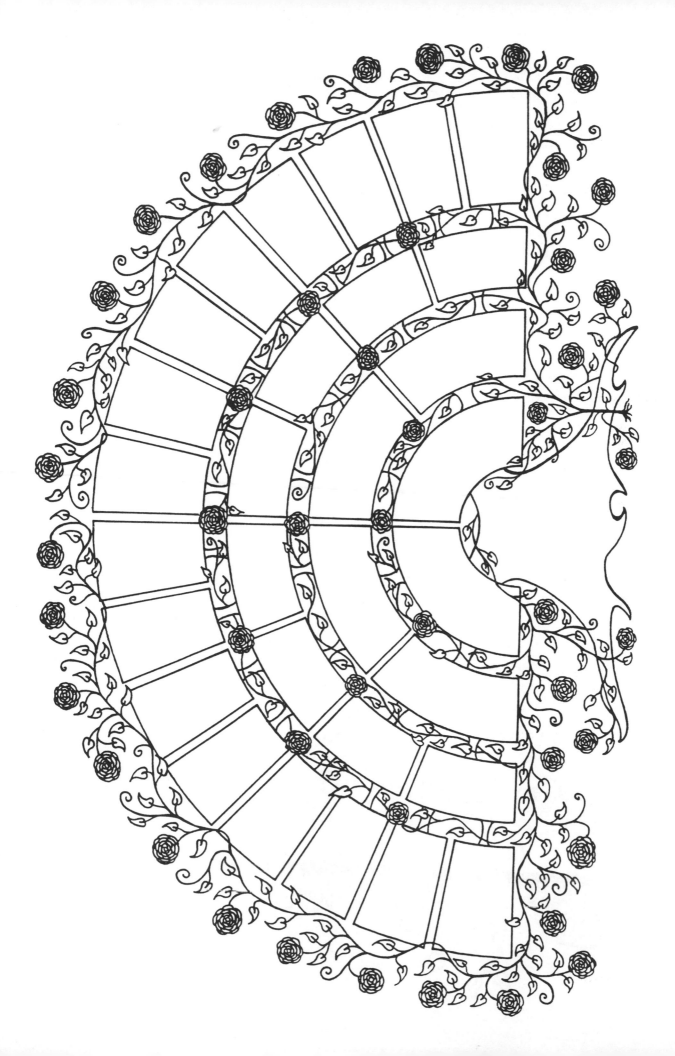

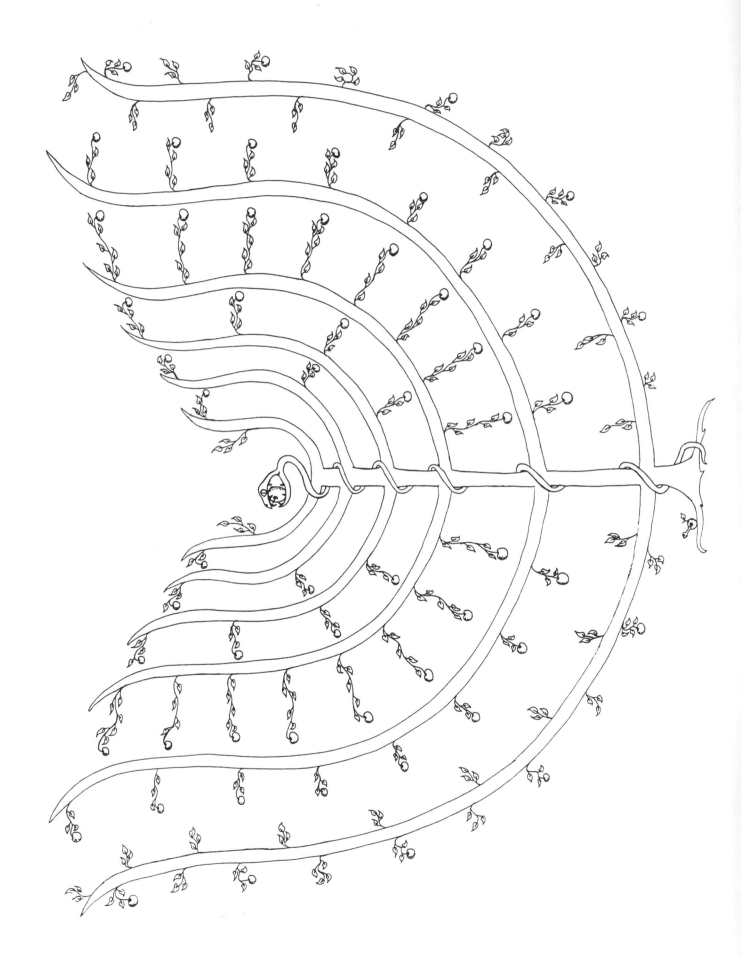

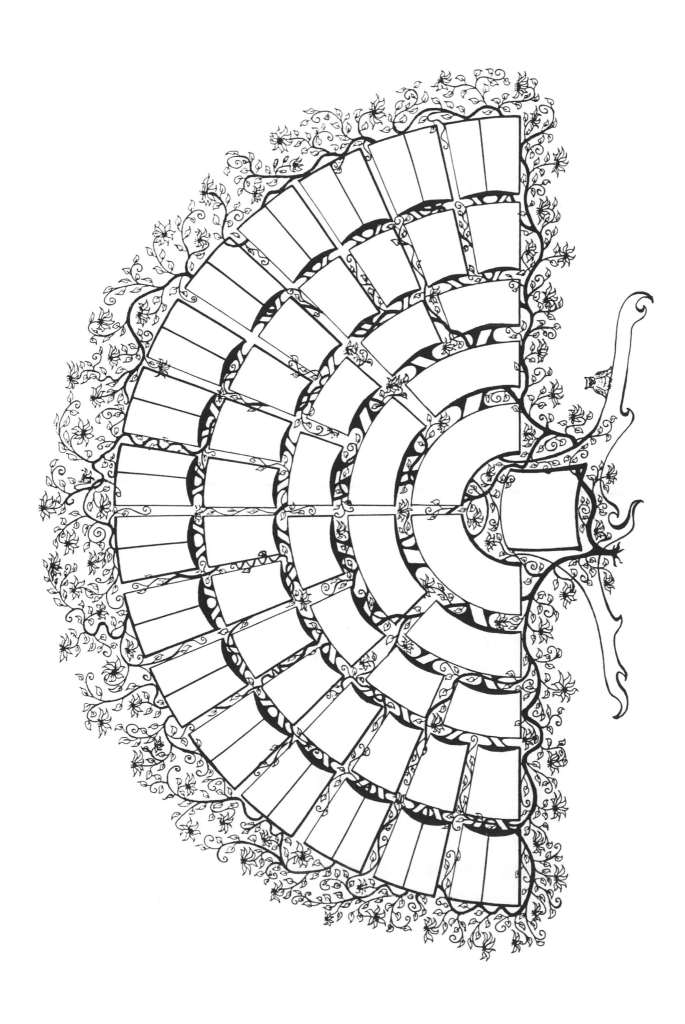

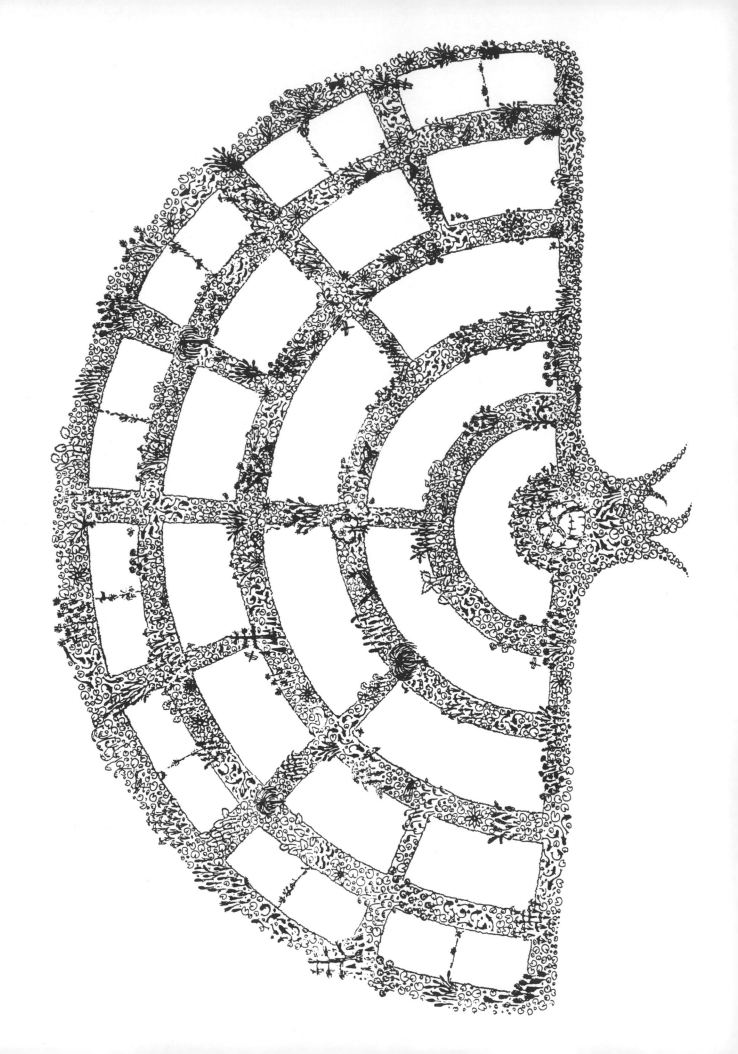

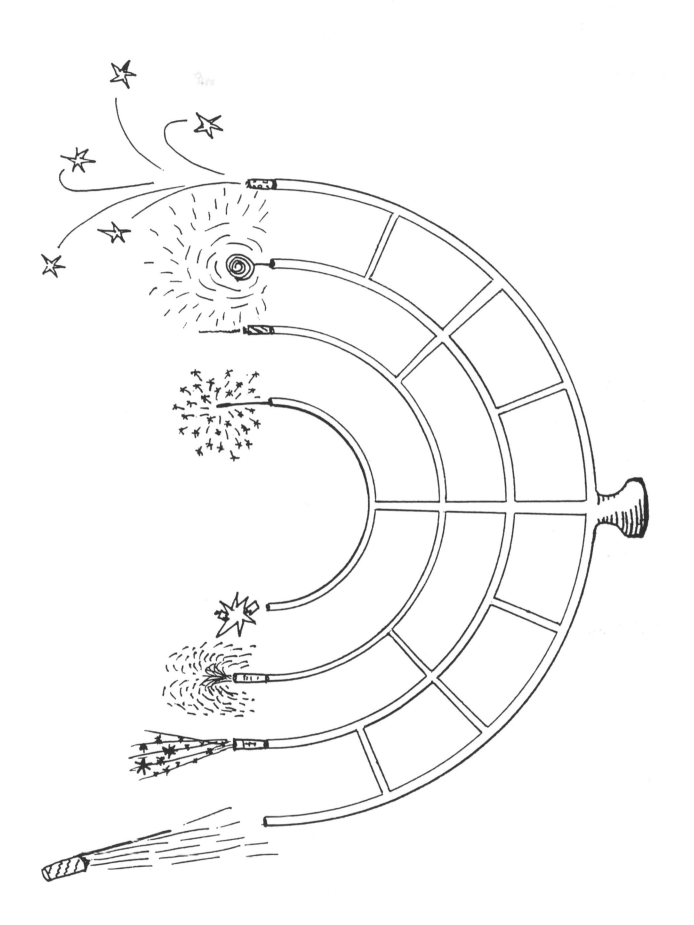

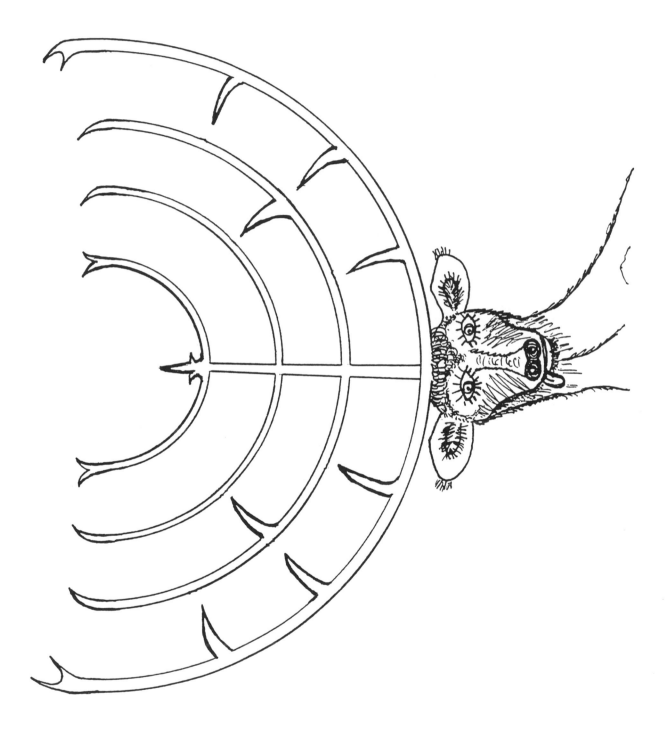

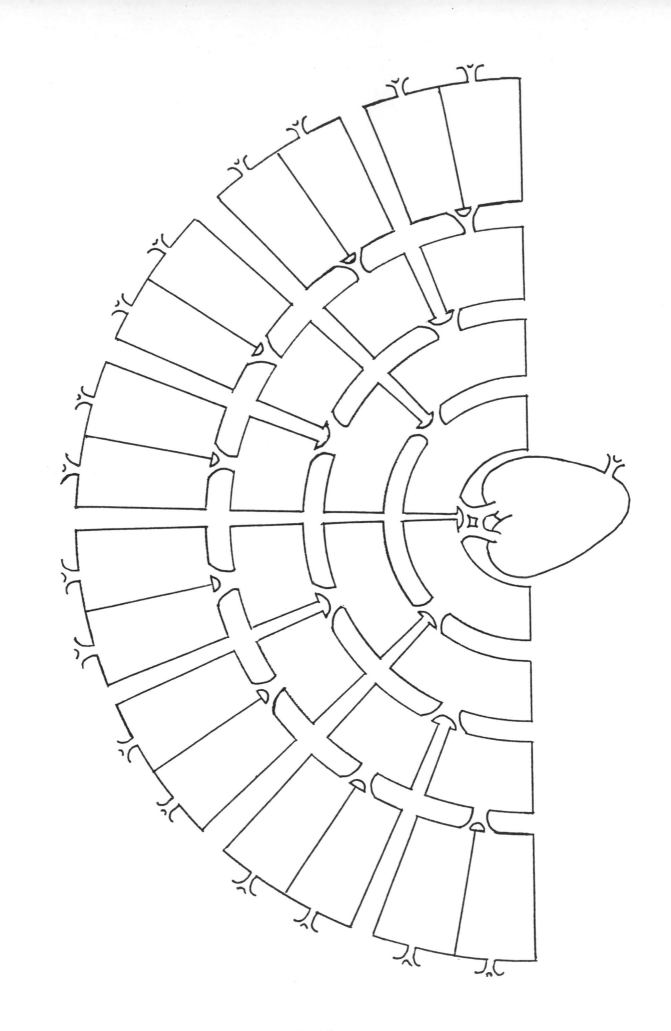

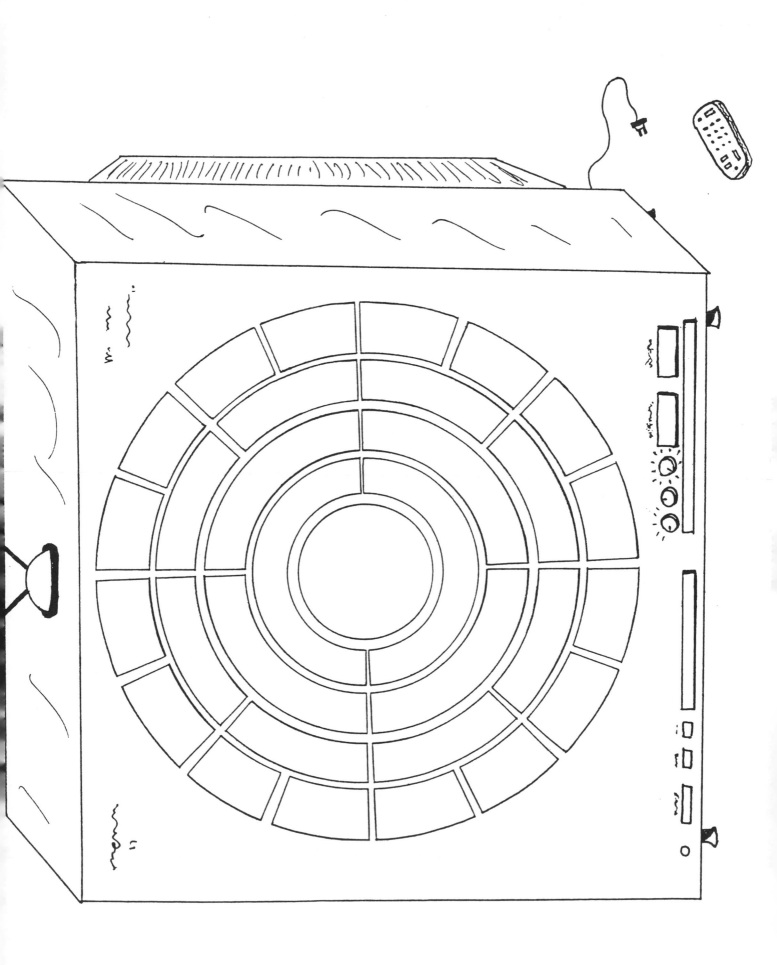

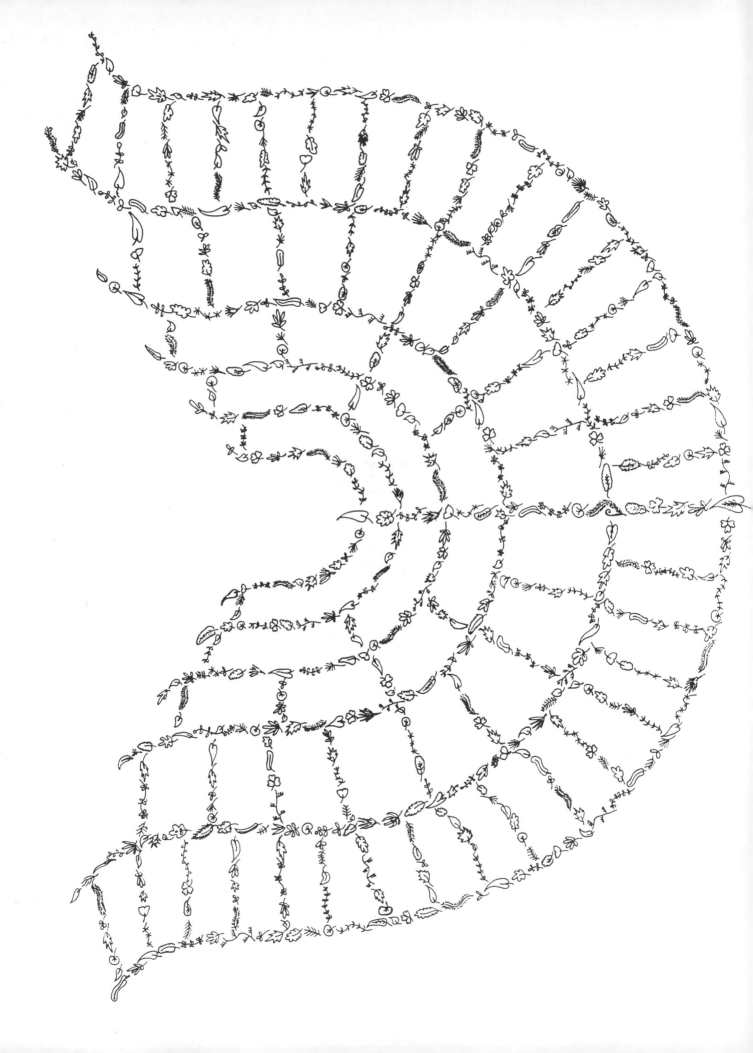